MIDLAND RAILWAY

PORTRAIT

CONTENTS

PETER TRUMAN & DAVID HUNT

Published jointly by Platform 5 Publishing Ltd., Lydgate House, Lydgate Lane, Sheffield S10 5FH and Foxline Publishing, 32 Urwick Road, Romiley, Stockport SK6 3JS.

Printed by Amadeus Press, 517 Leeds Road, Huddersfield HD2 1YJ.

ISBN 0 906579 72 4

ACKNOWLEDGEMENTS

This book would never have appeared but for the help and encouragement of many people. In particular, we would like to thank the following members of the Midland Railway Society for their contributions: Richard Betts, Laurence Knighton, Adrian Tester, Andrew Brown, John Childs, Jeff Dove, Tony Cripps, Geoff Grandfield, Steve Myers, Adrian Prescott, Peter Bunce, Roy Spalding, David Tee, David White, Peter Smith and Ken Woodhead. In addition we must thank many other organisations and individuals for their help, namely: Roger Carpenter, John Edgington, D.G. Geldard, Colin Maggs, Brian Miller, Tom Mott, Tim Shuttleworth, Bill Stubbs, James Turnbull, Glyn Waite, Gloucester Library, Lens of Sutton, Luton Museum, the Public Records Office and the Science Museum.

There is, however, one person who must be singled out for his assistance, support and encouragement. Our good friend Bob Essery has often gone out of his way to provide much-needed advice and assistance and without his help the book would probably never have seen the light of day.

To Jackie Statham we owe our thanks for rescuing us from months of two-fingered typing and helping with the organisation, and last but not least thanks to our wives Annie and Jill for putting up with the whole thing.

Peter Truman   David Hunt

Matlock, 1989   Boston, 1989

Frontispiece. King's Norton, 1910, northbound morning express, probably the 8.05 a.m. Bristol to Derby, is seen passing through this station. The train would be conveying through carriages for York and probably Bradford also. The station buildings on the left are a motley collection, this being unusual for the Midland, a company with a tradition of architectural appreciation. *W. Rear Collection*

Back Cover. A fine example of a Fred Taylor poster showing the interior of St. Pancras sometime between 1910 and 1920. There is a wealth of detail in the picture which can be considered as showing the latest practice of the day. *BR*

Midland Workhorse. One of Kirtley's legion of 0–6–0s, rebuilt by Johnson, takes a train of empty coal wagons up the Lickey incline. *R.J. Essery Collection*

INTRODUCTION

Hamilton Ellis said that the Midland was a magnificent railway, and so it was. To most people the very words "Midland Railway" conjure up a picture of a sparkling crimson locomotive, probably of Johnson origin, thundering through spectacular mountain scenery at the head of a stately rake of clerestory carriages, but the Midland was much more. Much has been written about that splendid and often controversial undertaking and there are volumes as yet unwritten, so why has this particular book appeared? It is not a definitive history of the railway, nor does it have a particular theme. There are no learned treatises on the Midland's impact on society, no examinations of the great figures of history who made it what it was – Stephenson, Hudson, Ellis, Allport, Kirtley, Clayton, Johnson and the rest; the enthusiast will not find detailed drawings of the products of Derby works, so what is its purpose? It merely tries to give an impression of what the Midland Railway was. Few, if any, who read this book will ever have seen a Midland train and fewer yet will clearly remember the experience. So we, who never knew the Midland but hold for it an affection as if it was a childhood friend, will try to portray something of what we understand by the words "The Midland Railway".

From its earliest beginnings to its demise as a separate entity the Midland strove to grow, to improve its services, and to present to the world an image of splendid and efficient reliability. Even in the days of the dreaded "parliamentary" carriages the Midland could never bring itself to approach the depths of functional austerity which some lines plumbed. Later on it led the way in comfort and convenience for passengers, even the third class to which some companies never quite managed to pay lip service. The admission of third class passengers to all trains in 1872 and the abolition of the second class in 1875 brought about a revolution in travel second only to the railway itself, and once more brought the Midland into the spotlight of controversy – a habit it never quite managed to break. From the inception of its oldest component-the Leicester and Swannington – to its apparent take over of the LMS, the Midland was nearly always involved in some controversy or other.

The Hudson inspired amalgamation of 1844 which produced the Midland; the acquisition of the Birmingham and Gloucester and Bristol and Gloucester which brought the standard gauge into the broad gauge hinterland; the building of the Peak Forest line dragging with it Ruskin's "close clinging damnation" into the bitterly defended North Western bastion at Manchester; the savage battle to build the once abandoned Settle and Carlisle and by way of those bleak moors bring Clayton's tall clerestories into Scotland – the list is long, too long to examine in detail here. There were other less glamorous but vastly important aspects of the Midland's progress. The introduction of brick arch fireboxes by Markham and Kirtley making coal a viable fuel; the early use of steel rails following trials at Derby; the Newark brake trials of 1875; pioneer train control systems, all of which added to the Midland's prosperity and popularity, were part of the company's drive and ambition.

Of course, the Midland was not pre-eminent in all it did, nor did all its activites endear it to everyone. Its two most infamous policies, those of persisting with Pintsch gas lighting and using small engines, condemned 33 passengers to death at Cudworth, Hawes Junction and Ais Gill, but then most railways had more fatalities than the Midland.

So what was the Midland Railway? Was it sweeping main lines through the backbone of England or small pastoral branches? Was it small green and polished brass locomotives pulling a collection of 4 wheeled carriages at a sedate trot or a Compound hurling itself and its crimson train at the Westmorland hills? Was it a seemingly endless coal train clattering southbound out of Toton behind a handful of Mr. Kirtley's 0–6–0s which went on forever, or was it a pick up goods pottering around Brecon? It was, of course, all these things and many more besides, and a full description would be to write a detailed history of the Midland Railway's 79 glorious years. With any luck it will never die as long as people can look at photographs which evoke the atmosphere of its greatness and hear in the mind the eldritch shriek of an express or the clash of loose coupled wagons. That is what this book is all about – the atmosphere of the Midland.

Hamilton Ellis was right – the Midland was a magnificent railway.

Plate 1. (facing page top) Midland Railway Royal train engine No. 495, one of Fowler's '483' class of 1912. Theoretically this locomotive was a rebuild of No. 154 – one of Johnson's '156' class built at Derby in 1897. Like many of the Midland's rebuilds, however, any resemblance to its former condition is hard to discern, and the supposed rebuilding was more a device to replace old locomotives out of the revenue account than a reflection of mechanical reality. *BR*

Plate 2. (facing page bottom) Sweeping main lines. One of Johnson's 'Belpaire' 4–4–0 s, No. 727, heads south along the Cromford to Whatstandwell section of the Peak Forest line with a rake of clerestory-roofed carriages in June 1911. To many this scene is the essence of the Midland. *BR*

Plate 3. Wagons galore! Coal and mineral traffic was a major source of income, and the massive coal trains snaking south from Toton to Cricklewood were a common sight. In this view, taken on 14th February 1910, Toton (Chilwell) sidings are crammed with both Midland and private owner wagons waiting their turn to join the exodus. *BR*

Plate 4. The Midland made extensive use of 0–4–4 tank locomotives, the type being equally at home on main line stopping trains and branch line services. This delightful view shows No. 1393, one of Johnson's designs, leaving Beauchief Station on a Chesterfield line train *circa* 1910. The pristine condition of the locomotive is noteworthy. These engines continued to do such work for many years after the Midland ceased to exist as a separate entity. *D.J. White Collection*

Plate 5. In the wake of the pick-up goods. Lenton goods shed in April 1922 showing unloaded Midland and LSWR wagons and a Midland horse drawn dray. The station platform just beyond the goods shed has been cut back as Lenton was closed to passengers on 1st July 1911 owing to competition from trams! Note the wagon turntable under the front axle of the LSWR wagon. *BR*

Plate 6. Classical Midland. A Spinner, a Compound and clerestory coaches comprise a down express just north of Elstree tunnel in 1920. Midland locomotive development failed to match the increase in train sizes in the 20th Century and piloting was endemic. Even the fabled compounds, the Midland's largest and most powerful engines, were frequently piloted as in this view of No. 1042 being assisted by Johnson single No. 672, itself a top link express locomotive 25 years earlier. *Authors' Collection*

Plate 7. Pastoral branches. Unlike many pre-grouping companies, the Midland did not possess many branch lines. Those it did have, however, contained some beautifully picturesque settings epitomised by this view of Nailsworth *circa* 1904. *Lens of Sutton*

THE MIDLAND SYSTEM

The Midland Railway was always centred on Derby. It was formed by the amalgamation of three companies radiating from the town – the Midland Counties, the Birmingham & Derby Junction, and the North Midland. Cut throat competition for London bound traffic by the first two, and higher than expected running costs for the last mentioned had led to financial problems for all three and the stage was set for George Hudson, a director of the North Midland, to propose amalgamation and have himself nominated chairman of the new undertaking.

Royal assent was received on 10th May 1844 and the Midland Railway Company officially came into being on 1st July of that year. The extremities of its system at that time were Leeds, Birmingham and Rugby but the "Railway King" had expansionist ideas and his board ably supported him. The Leicester & Swannington and the Sheffield & Rotherham soon joined the Derby camp and some opportunistic dealing by James Ellis following a chance meeting in a railway carriage snatched the Bristol–Birmingham line from under the vacillating Great Western's nose. One of Hudson's schemes to connect with his Great Eastern Railway and with the fledgling Great Northern at Bedford was seen by Parliament for the shady deal it was and rejected, but the 1847 bill to join the Great Northern at Hitchin was passed and so the Midland gained access to the Capital with its own trains into Kings Cross, albeit not until 1857.

Hudson's exposure and collapse in 1849 did relatively little damage to the Midland, mainly thanks to the integrity of Ellis and the rest of the board, and the company continued its policy of expansion. Severe congestion south of Hitchin and unacceptable delays via the London & North Western into Scotland gave impetus to two of the Midland's most celebrated lines – the London extension and the Settle & Carlisle opened in 1867 and 1876 respectively. The year 1867 also saw the Peak Forest line open to New Mills where a junction with the Manchester Sheffield & Lincolnshire Railway gave access to Manchester. In 1880 the line from New Mills South Junction to Manchester Central gave the Midland its own route throughout. The Midland system on the mainland was completed in 1912 when it acquired the London, Tilbury & Southend Railway, but it must be remembered that its activities reached further afield, for in 1903 it acquired the Belfast & Northern Counties Railway.

The Midland was also involved in more joint lines than any other British railway company and was the only one to own, wholly or partly, tracks in England, Scotland, Wales and Ireland.

The map opposite shows the extent of the Midland system in England and Wales as at January 1923 when its 2170 route miles passed into the hands of the London, Midland & Scottish Railway. Only the London & North Western and Great Western railways exceeded the Midland's route mileage and the Midland's goods and mineral traffic was greater in volume than that of either of them.

Plate 8. The staff at Derby station *circa* 1900. It would appear that juniors were not of sufficient status to be included! Apart from the policemen in the back row there are all grades from the station master to porters in evidence-the gentlemen in "mufti" in the second row being an unknown quantity. *M.L. Knighton Collection*

THE MIDLAND RAILWAY

AND JOINT LINES

IN ENGLAND AND WALES

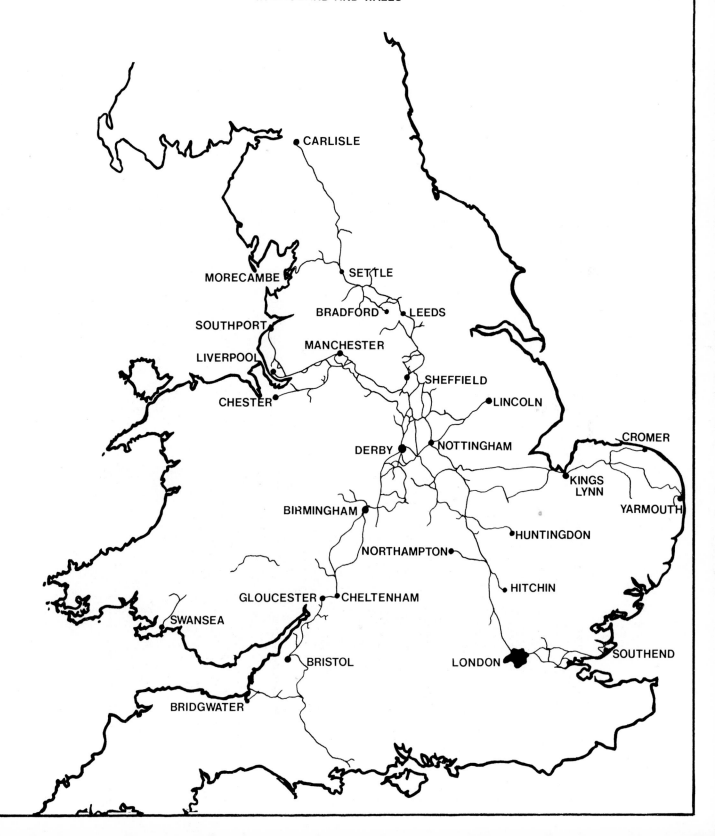

STAFF

When the railway age began there was no precedent for the vast numbers of people required for a single undertaking except the military. Thus the organisation of the railway workforce developed along closely military lines, even to the extent of being uniformed. Considering the scope for human precipitated disaster which the railways presented, the inherent discipline was an important aspect of the system whilst the reliance on laid down procedures and rules enabled a hitherto largely bucolic workforce to cope with a new and rapidly advancing technology. Of course, the railways did not escape the trials and tribulations of the industrial revolution and over the years working conditions, long hours and wages have all been the subjects of bitter dispute. Despite this, however, contemporary writers make frequent reference to the sense of pride with which the everyday running of the railways was undertaken, and it is inconceivable that the Midland could have achieved its reputation without a loyal and dedicated staff.

No portrait of the Midland, therefore, could be considered complete without acknowledging the people who made it all possible, though photographs of staff grades other than as incidentals to the main subject matter are much rarer than we would wish. We have therefore been fortunate in obtaining the pictures in this section and hope they serve as a reminder that a railway was only as good as the people who ran it and as we have said before, the Midland was a magnificent railway.

Plate 9. (right) One of the less common views of a footplate crew taken from the tender of a Kirtley 2–4–0 in the 1890s. At one time drivers tended to wear quite individual apparel even to the extent of white coats and top hats. By this date, however, the more uniform overalls and engineman's cap had taken over. It is likely that this photograph was an informal, unarranged one and thus gives a better impression of the day to day appearance of footplatemen than the more common posed type. *Authors' Collection*

Plate 10. (left) Photographs of footplate crews are relatively commonplace, but ones of the men who kept the locomotives running are much rarer. This picture shows some of the fitters and a foreman outside Derby works with a Kirtley '240' class 0–6–0, presumably in 1871 when the locomotive was being rebuilt. *R.J. Essery Collection*

RAILWAY FOOTBALL CLUB PARTINGTON CUP WINNERS 1909

Plate 11. We believe that this picture shows the football team from the Midland staff at Buxton and are including it as a reminder that there was a life outside the boundary fence. Apart from the legend "Railway Football Club Partington Cup Winners 1909", and the names of the players on the back of the original, we have no further information - if any reader can supply some we would be extremely interested. The players' names read as follows:

A. Pearson, J. Boywer, F. Poyner, J. Beard, B. Allen, Brocklehurst, W. Bosley, J. Farlam , F. Martin, W. Fanshaw, F. Gladwin.

P.Cook Collection

Plate 12. (left) Mr. Albert Edward Peacey (1858–1942). Born in Cheltenham, Mr. Peacey joined the Midland Railway *circa* 1875 and quickly rose to be a top link guard successively at Bradford, Liverpool and Manchester. Between 1885 and 1914 he worked as a through guard between Manchester Victoria and Glasgow St. Enoch – hence the cap badge and collar tabs reading "Midland & G & SW........ Through Guard". Such duties ceased at the outbreak of the 1914–18 war and Carlisle became the northern limit of Midland working. Mr. Peacey retired in 1923 after 48 years' service on the railway. *O. Carter Collection*

Plate 13. (centre left) An inspector (left) and a ticket collector apparently posed by the enamelled nameboard and "unclimbable" iron railings at Luton station around the turn of the century. Whether the grim expressions are part of the pose or a natural result of many years dealing with the travelling public is not known!
Luton Museum & Art Gallery

Plate 14. (right) During the 1914–18 war large numbers of hitherto men's jobs were taken over by women as many workers joined the armed forces. Most staff grades except footplate ones had an influx of women. This photograph shows a group of cleaners by a grounded Pullman sleeping car body at Hellifield in 1916.
Authors' Collection

Plates 15 & 16. The staff at Addingham Station, on the Skipton to Ilkley line, on two separate occasions around the turn of the century. Based purely on the appearance of the characters common to both pictures we would place Plate 15 (facing page) as the earlier of the two, although there is probably no more than a couple of years or so between them. The neatness and cleanliness of the station and equipment is self evident. *D.J. White Collection*

LOCOMOTIVES

Only four men were ever in charge of the Midland Railway's locomotive affairs – Matthew Kirtley, Samuel Johnson, Richard Deeley and Henry (later Sir Henry) Fowler. Each man's contribution to Midland locomotive development was as distinctive as his character, though responsibilities changed a good deal over the years. Whilst Kirtley was locomotive, carriage and wagon superintendent, Johnson succeeded only to the locomotive department. At the end of Deeley's relatively short term of office the responsibility for locomotive running was further split off and Fowler took over as the Midland's first, and only, Chief Mechanical Engineer.

Matthew Kirtley was born on 6th February 1813 at Tanfield in County Durham. He began his railway career as a fireman on the Warrington & Newton Railway then went as a driver to the Leeds & Selby and later to the London & Birmingham where he reputedly drove the first train to enter Euston. In May 1839 he became locomotive foreman at the Hampton in Arden shops of the Birmingham & Derby Junction Railway and was promoted to Locomotive Superintendent in June 1842. On the formation of the Midland Railway, Hudson appointed Matthew locomotive, carriage and wagon superintendent in preference to Josiah Kearsley of the Midland Counties and his elder brother Thomas Kirtley of the North Midland. Immediately, Matthew Kirtley started to rationalise the rather motley assortment of locomotives the new concern had inherited. He began expanding the capacity of Derby Works towards locomotive construction rather than just maintenance and introduced some measure of standardisation. In 1851 Derby Works produced its first new locomotive, 0–6–0 No. 147, and year by year its production increased, though the Midland never became self sufficient in locomotive construction. Throughout Kirtley's reign, locomotive types were fairly standard. After some early 2–4–0s the goods locomotives were almost invariably 0–6–0s whilst passenger engines were initially 2–2–2s and later, and more predominantly 2–4–0s. Kirtley's locomotives were always built to last and a great many of them passed through the hands of his successors to be modified and rebuilt. The last, BR No. 58110, a '700' class 0–6–0 built in 1870, was not retired until 1951.

Kirtley died after a long illness in 1873, and was succeeded in the locomotive department by Samuel Waite Johnson. Born at Bramley near Leeds on 14th October 1831, Johnson was apprenticed to James Fenton, a partner in the locomotive building firm of E.B. Wilson & Co., and assisted Fenton and David Joy with the design of the famous "Jenny Lind" 2–2–2 express engines. From Wilson's he moved to the Great Northern Railway where he became an assistant district locomotive superintendent before leaving in 1859 to take up post as acting locomotive superintendent of the Manchester, Sheffield & Lincolnshire Railway. Simi-

lar appointments with the Edinburgh & Glasgow and Great Eastern Railways followed before he joined the Midland in Kirtley's stead. Johnson immediately began an extensive rebuilding and reboilering programme and further standardised the Midland's fleet.

He also introduced 0–4–4 tank and 0–6–0 tender locomotives very similar to his Great Eastern examples. In 1876 he began building 4–2–2s, to all intents and purposes stretched 2–4–0s, and then in 1887 he reintroduced the single driving wheel type, this time a 4–2–2, for express working with the benefit of steam sanding. He continued building 4–2–2s longer than anyone else, and the last one did not leave Derby Works until 1900. At the turn of the century, however, something bigger was needed and in 1900 he introduced his 'Belpaire' 4–4–0s, a departure from the Johnson tradition of stately Victorian elegance which many people viewed with aesthetic misgivings. In 1903 there appeared the first of the Compounds, generally held to be the only successful application of compound expansion to British steam locomotives. With one inside high pressure and two outside low pressure cylinders on the system patented by W.M. Smith, these engines were immensely successful and were the forerunners of the famous Midland Compounds. They were Johnson's swansong for he retired on the last day of 1903 and lived in Nottingham until his death in January 1912.

Richard Mountford Deeley was born on 24th October 1855 and after attending grammar school in Chester he went to work at the Hydraulic Engineering Co. in 1873 where he showed such promise that he was accepted as a pupil of Johnson's at the age of 20. He excelled at experimental work and in 1890 became head of the testing department. In 1893 he was appointed Inspector of Boilers, Engines and Machinery and was seen as being groomed for greatness. Within eighteen months of his succeeding to the post of Works Manager in 1902 he was additionally Electrical Engineer and Assistant Locomotive Superintendent, and on Johnson's retirement he became Locomotive Superintendent.

Deeley promptly set about bringing the Midland locomotive fleet into the twentieth century and embarked on a extensive reboilering and rebuilding of Johnson types. He is probably best remembered for his development of the compounds into the classic Midland design, his simplified livery of 1905, and the renumbering of Midland locomotives for the first time into a logical sequence in 1907. In 1909 the Midland board decided to divide the Locomotive Superintendent's post into two – Chief mechanical Engineer and Chief Motive Power Superintendent – and Deeley advised them that he felt this situation would be best met by appointing two new men in his stead. His resignation was accepted and he was awarded a substantial pension.

Deeley devoted the rest of his life to scientific

research until his death in 1944. Many stories abound concerning Deeley's resignation from the Midland – tales of bitter feuds over the Paget locomotive, ordering his nameplate removed from his office door and storming out of Derby Works etc., but we can find no reason for supposing they are anything but apocryphal. The Midland's one and only CME was Henry Fowler. Born at Evesham in 1870 he entered the service of the Lancashire & Yorkshire Railway, leaving in 1900 to join the Midland as Gas Engineer and Chief of the Testing Department. In 1905 he became Assistant Works Manager.

He had just become Works Manager when Deeley resigned and another promotion followed. Between the years 1915 and 1919 Fowler was employed by the Ministry of Munitions, for which he received his Knighthood in 1918, thus his active control of Midland locomotive affairs only amounted to nine years.

Plate 17. Photographs of Kirtley locomotives in their original (or nearly original) condition are not commonplace. This picture shows Sharp Stewart & Co built single No. 124 more or less as built in 1853. The tender appears to have received a larger tank than originally provided and the locomotive is unusual for its type in having no tie bars on the outside frames and in being left hand drive – most Midland locomotives were driven from the right. The short springs and small clearance between the axleboxes and the tops of the hornguides are poor features of the design. No. 124 was renumbered 124A in December 1874. *Authors' Collection*

MIDLAND LOCOMOTIVE NUMBERING

Throughout this book there are many references to locomotives being renumbered, sometimes several times. For those not properly acquainted with the vagaries of the Midland, a few notes on the subject are in order.

In the earliest Midland days goods and passenger locomotives were numbered in separate blocks, and this generally held good. Classes, however, would often start with an orderly sequence in an allocated number block then run out of room and be allocated numbers left vacant in other blocks or those of withdrawn locomotives. Sometimes such mavericks would be subsequently moved into their own class block if a number became available, or renumbered to make way for new locomotives. Additionally there was the duplicate list, primarily an accounting exercise for locomotives stored out of use or declared surplus to capital stock, which used the A suffix. Some locomotives actually carried more than one duplicate number and some were restored to the capital list – being renumbered in the process!

In 1907 Deeley brought method into the Midland's locomotive list and renumbered the entire fleet. The oldest passenger tender engine was numbered 1, the oldest (in theory) passenger tank engine 1198 and the oldest tender goods engine 2200. Suitable gaps were left to ensure that sufficient space would be available for new locomotives.

In most instances in this book the full numbering history of a locomotive has been omitted as too tedious. Details can be found in the "Midland Locomotives" series published by Wild Swan.

Plate 18. Among the thirteen locomotives which the Midland took over when it absorbed the Little North Western in 1852 were three 2–2–2 well tanks built by Fairbairn & Sons such as the one here illustrated. The location is unknown – it resembles Tewkesbury but the brickwork to the right of the picture is not quite right. This type of locomotive was also supplied to Brazil and one is preserved there.
Authors' Collection

Plate 19. The North Western well tank *Competitor* was built in 1851, becoming Midland No. 159 in 1852 and, like its two sisters, was rebuilt as an 0–4–2 in January 1865. After a further rebuilding it was renumbered 202 and was photographed between 1877 and 1890. Later renumbered 2065A, it was withdrawn in 1892.
Authors' Collection

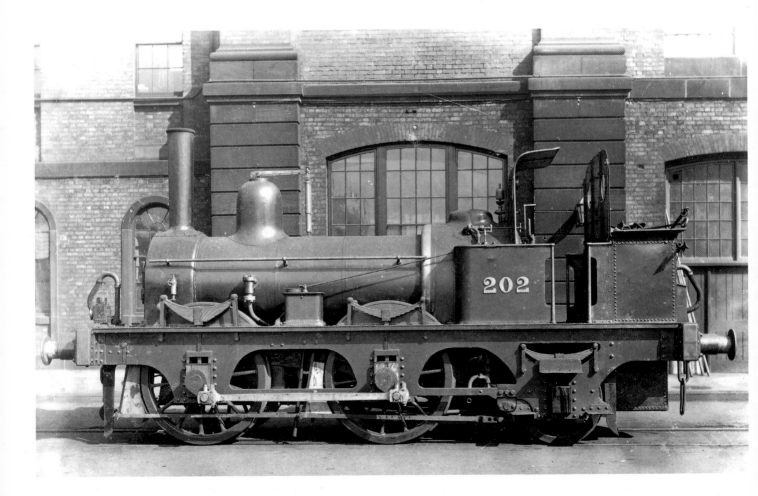

Plate 20. The '1070' class was Kirtley's last design of 2–4–0 though they were not built until after his death. No. 1088, seen here at a location believed to be Millers Dale, was completed in 1875 and shows Johnson's influence. *BR*

Plate 21. The '240' class 0–6–0s were built in large numbers between 1850 and 1862. As built they exhibited many variations, even to the extent of the wheelbase changing between batches, and subsequent rebuilding by Johnson made things even more complicated. To many people, therefore, No. 557 built in 1858 is just a "straight framed Kirtley goods" with a Johnson tender. This locomotive carried many numbers in its lifetime starting with 189 and passing through 701 and 293, both in 1867, 293A in 1877, 557 in 1902 and finally 2348 in 1907. It was rebuilt in 1879 and 1894 and reboilered in 1915 only to be withdrawn four years later. *Authors' Collection*

Plate 22. Although the original glass plate was broken, this photograph of No. 695 is included as it shows a Kirtley 0–4–4 well tank (or back tank) soon after its completion in 1869. Six of these locomotives were built by Beyer Peacock & Co and were popular and successful. Note the equalising beam between the coupled axle springs – a common feature of Kirtley's designs. *A. Prescott Collection*

Plate 23. The '156' class 2–4–0 was one of Kirtley's most successful passenger designs. Built in the mid-1860s, many of them survived well into LMS days and one is preserved as No. 158A, currently at the Midland Railway Trust Centre at Butterley. No 104A, seen here in the mid-1890s, was built in 1867 and was withdrawn by the LMS in 1932. *Authors' Collection*

Plate 24. No. 2038A represents a class of locomotive with very varying antecedents. These 0–6–0 well tanks were officially all rebuilds, and for those which were formerly 0–6–0 goods engines this seems reasonable, but the ones which had previous incarnations as singles, or even Cramptons.......! No 2038A became a well tank in 1867 and was withdrawn in 1906. *BR*

Plate 25. Most of Johnson's 280 0–6–0 side tank shunting engines were built with open back cabs (or "half cabs" as they are sometimes incorrectly called) though some were subsequently rebuilt with enclosed cabs. Forty of the type, however, were built with such cabs including No. 1136. Note the elaborate lining out of the period. *R.J. Essery Collection*

M. R. Modern Goods Locomotive

Plate 26. In 1897 the caption on this postcard view would have been correct – No. 2261 was built in that year and represented the latest type of Johnson 0–6–0 goods locomotive. The photograph shows to good effect the elegant lines of Johnson's designs and the decorative though not overfussy lining out. We were interested to find that the postcard was not posted until 1947! *Authors' Collection*

Plate 27. Samuel Johnson was also responsible for the locomotives of the Midland & Great Northern Joint Railway. Neilson's built some 0–6–0s for the M & GN virtually identical to Johnson's latest design for the Midland as can be seen by comparing this picture of No. 59, completed in 1896, with No. 2261 in Plate 26.
Authors' Collection

Plate 28. In the opinion of the authors the early Johnson 4–4–0s were amongst the most elegant designs ever produced. It is a great pity that colour photography was not commonplace when this picture of No. 1814 was taken. What a sight it must have made at the head of a rake of Clayton's clerestory carriages.
D.F. Tee Collection

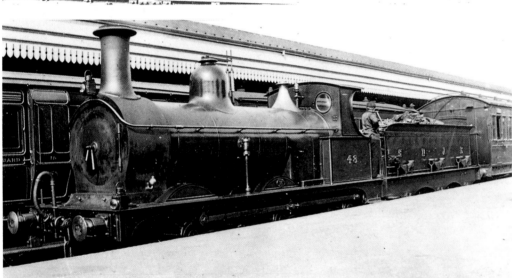

Plate 29. The Somerset & Dorset's locomotive fleet also came under Johnson's jurisdiction and included some of his 0–6–0s. No. 48 built by the Vulcan Foundry at Newton-le-Willows in 1884 was slightly smaller than the type illustrated in Plates 26 & 27 but the general lines and boiler fittings are unmistakably Johnson.
Authors' Collection

Plate 30. The "Spinners" were probably the most famous of Johnson's 19th century designs. The type was introduced in 1887 and by the end of 1900 ninety-five had been built to several slightly different designs. The basic shape remained similar but over that period the engines became gradually larger in terms of driving wheel diameter, cylinder size etc. This view illustrates No. 181 at Cheltenham on a Bradford to Bristol express *circa* 1903. This particular example was built in 1897 which represents the intermediate design of Johnson 4–2–2 with 7 ft. 6 in. diameter driving wheels. The 2–4–0 in the background is in a bay platform used by trains of the Midland and South Western Junction Railway.
Authors' Collection

Plate 31. To one of the authors the last batch of 7 ft. 9½ in. singles were aesthetically the epitome of Midland locomotive design. As well as the increase in driving wheel diameter their boilers were larger than previous batches and the domes were moved back to the middle ring. Like the '700' class Belpaire 4–4–0s and the first batch of Compounds they were coupled to large "Water cart" bogie tenders as the Midland at that time lacked water troughs. In the case of the singles these tenders weighed more than the locomotives when fully loaded. No. 21 was built in 1900 as one of the 'Princess of Wales' class. *Authors' Collection*

Plate 32. (above) At the other end of the Johnson locomotive spectrum were his small 0–4–0 saddle tank shunting engines. As can be seen from this photograph not all Midland locomotives were as well kept and cared for as the singles, though beneath the grime 1507 is lined out like its more elegant brethren. The different pattern spokes give the engine a curious appearance.
Authors' Collection

Plate 33. (above) This view shows to advantage the cab layout of a typical Johnson 0–6–0. The firedoor design was generally liked by firemen as the main door could be left closed and the fire fed through the 4 in. deep upper door, thus preventing the fire from being overcooled and providing a good supply of secondary air where it was required during firing. Until the knack of firing through this gap was discovered, however, bruised knuckles were an occupational hazard. *R.C. Betts Collection*

Plate 34. (below) The '1883' class was the most numerous of Johnson's 0–6–0s. No. 1961 was photographed at Hasland between 1904 and 1906 specially decorated for an unknown occasion. The headboard reads "Hasland, Westhouses and Staveley" and the picture on the leading tender panel appears to be of Robert Burns. Several similar photographs exist which suggest that the occasion was a regular event. *G.G. Grandfield Collection*

Plate 35. One of Deeley's passenger locomotive designs was that of the 'Flatiron' 0–6–4 tanks, so called because of their heavy, slablike appearance. They had mixed success and were said by some contemporary observers to be poor steamers. The steam passages were somewhat convoluted which may explain the poor draughting from which they supposedly suffered. They were built in 1907 in the form shown in this photograph of 2011 taken at Stafford in 1921. They were all superheated by the LMS but even then do not appear to have achieved much success and were relegated to secondary duties before being scrapped in the early 1930s. They were apparently responsible for some serious derailments, but this appears to be after they were rebuilt by the LMS. No. 2011 was one of six locomotives fitted with Westinghouse equipment for trials on the LT & S but the experiment was not a success and they were returned to the Midland system proper in 1914. *B.J. Miller Collection*

Plate 36. The '4F' class was the last type of Midland goods locomotive. Known as the "big goods" they were mainly built by Armstrong Whitworth & Co. No. 3835 was the first of the class and was built to order No. 4000 in 1911. Its sister engine, 3836, was built to order No. 4001 in the same year and until 1917 no further examples appeared. By the time of the grouping, however, 147 had been built and all survived into BR days. The design was also adopted by the LMS which built left hand drive versions. The first two locomotives originally had steam reversing gear but this was not a success and was removed in 1923; no other 4Fs were so fitted. *Authors' Collection*

Plate 38. (above) The interior of, we believe, Hasland (Chesterfield) locomotive shed in the early 1890s showing a predominance of Kirtley 2–4–0s and 0–6–0s. The depot supplied locomotives for the vast numbers of southbound mineral trains and 0–6–0s formed the basis of its stud. The shed was a roundhouse type common on the Midland (despite being square!) and was coded No. 23. The picture shows details of the inspection pits, smoke ventilators and the covered turntable well. *G.G. Grandfield Collection*

Plate 37. (previous page) No. 4 Shed at Derby was opened in 1890 to overcome the chronic shortage of locomotive stabling space. The interior of the shed is seen here shortly after opening and, as can be seen, it was a double roundhouse with two turntable wells. In the left foreground is rebuilt '890' class 2–4–0 No. 891 whilst behind it is S & DJR 0–6–0 No. 60, only just completed in July 1890. The '890' class 2–4–0 No. 132 on the right is in an earlier state of rebuilding than No. 891 and behind it is '480' class 0–6–0 NO. 484A, placed on the duplicate list in June 1879. Next to the back of the shed on the right hand side is one of the last unrebuilt Kirtley 0–6–0s with Kirtley boiler fittings and "baker's oven" smokebox doors. *Authors' Collection*

Plate 39. By the turn of the century even Johnson was replacing aesthetics with functionality in his designs and the 'Belpaires' were probably his least attractive 4–4–0s. They were large engines by Midland standards of the time and, in common with the later batches of 4–2–2s, many were originally coupled to large bogie tenders of upwards of 4000 gallons capacity. No. 719 was built in 1902 (originally numbered 2790) and rebuilt into the form shown here by Fowler. *W.J. Reynolds*

Plate 40. The Compounds were probably the most famous Midland locomotives of all. From the original five Johnson examples of 1902/3 Deeley developed the classical Midland Compound and by the grouping the class numbered 45 locomotives. Fowler started rebuilding them with superheated G9As boilers in 1913, but by 1923 only 24 had been so treated and it was not until 1928 that the last saturated engine was modified. The LMS adopted the design with a number of detail differences and they were to be found all over its system. They proved to be long lived engines and the last one was not withdrawn by BR until 1961. No. 1030 was built in 1906 as No. 1025 and was not fitted with the superheated boiler until 1925. It was withdrawn in 1951 as BR No. 41030. The first of the class, No. 1000 (1907 numbering) is preserved at the National Railway Museum, York in a close approximation to its 1914 superheated condition. *Authors' Collection*

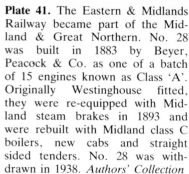

Plate 41. The Eastern & Midlands Railway became part of the Midland & Great Northern. No. 28 was built in 1883 by Beyer, Peacock & Co. as one of a batch of 15 engines known as Class 'A'. Originally Westinghouse fitted, they were re-equipped with Midland steam brakes in 1893 and were rebuilt with Midland class C boilers, new cabs and straight sided tenders. No. 28 was withdrawn in 1938. *Authors' Collection*

Plate 42. One of the renowned Tilbury tanks, in this instance No. 7, built by Sharp, Stewart & Co in 1880 to a design supervised by William Adams of the Great Eastern. As built, No. 7 had steam brakes but was later fitted with Westinghouse equipment. It was also one of four engines fitted with condensing apparatus and shorter chimneys for working over the Metropolitan District lines to Whitechapel in 1902 and in 1904 the cab profile was modified because of restricted tunnel clearance. Unfortunately their troglodyte existence also involved these engines being painted black instead of the ornate green LT & S livery. After electrification of the District in 1905 No. 7 returned to normal working but retained its condensing gear until 1919 when it was also painted Midland red. It was numbered 2116 under MR ownership and withdrawn by the LMS in 1935. *Authors' Collection*

Plate 43. The last design of locomotive for the LT & SR by R.H. Whitelegg was for a class of large Baltic tanks built by Beyer, Peacock & Co. They were big engines weighing 94 tons and were to have carried running numbers 87–94. Before they were delivered, however, the LT & SR was taken over by the Midland, which promptly tried to sell the big 4–6–4s, and they were tried out by both the Great Western and SECR but were rejected by both. Eventually the Midland gave in and took them into stock as Nos 2100–2107 a year after Beyer Peacock delivered them in 1912. They were visually very similar to Whitelegg's Glasgow & South Western Railway Baltics. From time to time they were tried on other parts of the Midland system but did not appear to offer any advantage over native types. *Authors' Collection*

PASSENGER TRAVEL

It has often been said that the railways were conceived and built for mineral and goods traffic, that the enthusiasm of people to travel on trains caught the railways by surprise, and that they never recovered from that surprise and learned to cope with the travelling public. Whether this is true or not, it has to be admitted by even the most ardent railway enthusiast that some lines at some times treated their fare paying passengers abominably. One of the Midland's strengths was its propensity for improving the lot of its passengers before the opposition. Whilst acknowledging that business acumen rather than philanthropy was the motivation, we would suggest that the ordinary railway traveller in the 19th and early 20th centuries had cause to be grateful to the Midland as the other companies were more or less forced to follow Derby's lead. The introduction of Pullman cars and the admission of third class passengers to all trains were moves which caused stirs in boardrooms throughout the country, but the abolition of the

second class in 1875, with the resultant improvement in third class travel, was a master stroke which caused a veritable storm.

By the turn of the century the Midland's reputation for comfort was pre-eminent; whether a passenger was travelling one stop on a country branch, commuting into Moorgate via the widened lines, or setting out from St. Pancras bound for Carlisle or beyond, he could reasonably expect that the Midland Railway would convey him in timely and comfortable safety.

The vehicles in which the Midland accommodated its customers were varied and to make any general pronouncement about the appearance of a Midland passenger train is extremely difficult. To say that they were nearly all clerestoried, double headed or little but often (all of which have been said in print!) is obviously the worst kind of sweeping generalisation and quite untrue. One of the intentions of this section, therefore, is to give some idea of the variety of trains in which the Midland conveyed its public.

Plate 44. A remarkable variety of roofs, profiles and footboards is evident on this eleven coach express heading towards St. Pancras *circa* 1905 behind an unidentified Johnson 4–4–0 being piloted by a rebuilt Kirtley '890' class 2–4–0. Locomotive development to keep pace with growing train size is illustrated by the fact that the pilot engine seen here was built for the Scotch express traffic in the mid-1870s and superseded by the train engine before it too was demoted by the 'Belpaires' and the first Compounds by the time this picture was taken. *L & GRP courtesy David & Charles*

Plate 45. This official posed photograph captures well the appearance of a typical Midland Scotch express in the last decade of the 19th century. The locomotive, No. 145, is one of Johnson's celebrated 'Spinners', so called either because of their tendency to slip on starting or because of the lack of outside rods made them appear to "spin" along the track; their nickname has been ascribed to both causes. It was the introduction of steam sanding which persuaded Johnson to re-introduce singles after they had been superseded by coupled locomotives for fast passenger traffic, and they were built at Derby as late as 1900. The mixture of four, six and eight-wheeled low roofed stock with two of the famous twelve-wheeled clerestories provides a rich harvest for modellers; the two six-wheelers are part of the Midland and Scottish Joint Stock. *BR*

Plate 46. A 4–4–0 and 48 ft. clerestories – to many this is the definitive Midland train. In this case No. 448 of the '483' class heads an express near Bentham on the Hellifield to Carnforth line just after the grouping in 1923. *D.J. White Collection*

Plate 47. For many years Johnson's 0–4–4 tank engines were the mainstay of suburban and branch line trains. Their acceleration enabled them to maintain even the most smartly-timed services. In this view Dübs built No. 2618 is seen running bunker first near Bentham with a rake of Bain clerestories. *Authors' Collection*

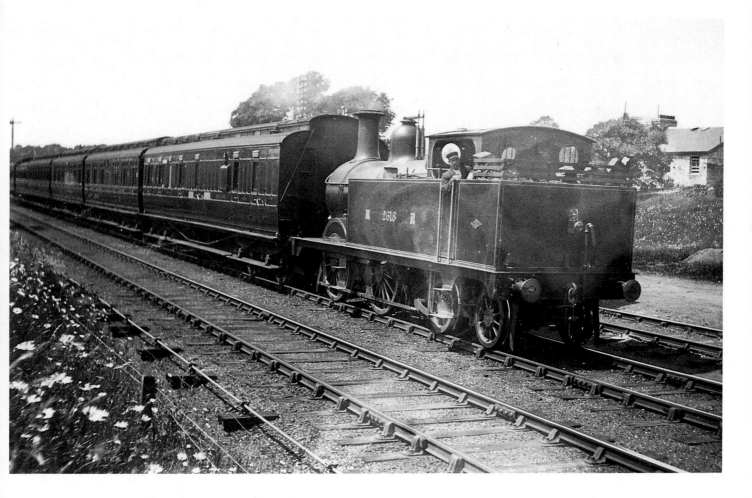

Plate 48. The Midland reached York by means of running powers over the North Eastern Railway. H boilered 4–4–0 No. 359 pulls out of York with an express composed of 13 ft. 1 in. and 13 ft. 3 in. high clerestories on 17th June 1922. *W.L. Good*

Plate 49. A 14 coach express of mixed stock double headed near Northfield in August 1921. The pilot engine is a '483' class 4–4–0 No. 494 built in 1912. The splash deflectors below the buffer beam were fitted to prevent the front bogie axleboxes from suffering the effects of spray when the locomotive was behind another which was picking up water from troughs. The train engine is a 'Belpaire' 4–4–0, No. 723, temporarily fitted for oil burning; one of the oil tanks can be seen above the top of the tender. *W.L. Good*

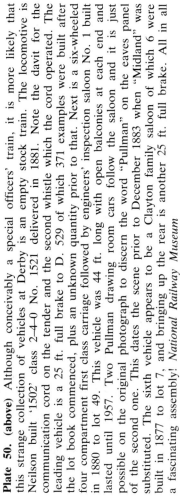

Plate 50. (above) Although conceivably a special officers' train, it is more likely that this strange collection of vehicles at Derby is an empty stock train. The locomotive is Neilson built '1502' class 2-4-0 No. 1521 delivered in 1881. Note the davit for the communication cord on the tender and the second whistle which the cord operated. The leading vehicle is a 25 ft. full brake to D. 529 of which 371 examples were built after the lot book commenced, plus an unknown quantity prior to that. Next is a six-wheeled four compartment first class carriage followed by engineers' inspection saloon No. 1 built in 1880 to lot 49. This vehicle was 44 ft. long with open balconies at each end and lasted until 1957. Two Pullman drawing room cars follow the saloon and it is just possible on the original photograph to discern the word "Pullman" on the eaves panel of the second one. This dates the scene prior to December 1883 when "Midland" was substituted. The sixth vehicle appears to be a Clayton family saloon of which 6 were built in 1877 to lot 7, and bringing up the rear is another 25 ft. full brake. All in all a fascinating assembly! *National Railway Museum*

Plate 51. (right) With a headcode indicating "ordinary passenger train", Kirtley '800' class 2-4-0 proceeds along the "Little" North Western line with the 5.30 p.m. Hellifield–Carnforth train in the summer of 1923. Although owned by the LMS the train still bears its Midland identity. Once again the profile is an up and down one with three clerestories and one arc-roofed carriage whilst a horsebox brings up the rear. *Authors' Collection*

Plate 52. An interesting view of Johnson 'Belpaire' 4–4–0 No. 767, running with No. 761's tender, on a down express for Leeds at Mill Hill. The picture illustrates well the difference in profile between earlier clerestory stock like the twelve-wheeler coach third from the engine, and the larger, later ones either side.
Authors' Collection

Plate 53. A 'flatiron' 0–6–4T is helped with its long train of arc-roofed bogie coaches near Halesowen Junction in May 1922. Its helper, 0–4–4 tank No. 1226, was the first of its type built by the Midland under the auspices of S.W. Johnson in 1875; originally it was No. 6. *W.L. Good*

Plate 54. This picture has a number of interesting aspects even though the clarity is not all we might wish. Firstly the locomotive, a Johnson 0–6–0, is a type normally associated with goods workings and its headboard, which reads "SOUTHEND", indicates that it is working over the London, Tilbury & Southend Railway. The headboard, however, is not the type normally seen in photographs of LT & SR trains. The explanation is that this picture was taken before the Midland absorbed the Tilbury but had running powers over the line.
R.J. Essery Collection

Plate 55. A rather picturesque photograph of a Kirtley '800' class 2-4-0 near Bentham with an assortment of Clayton and Bain carriages *circa* 1905. The "mixed" appearance of the train is exaggerated by the arc-roofed carriage towards the rear of the line of clerestories. *L & GRP*

Plate 56. (below) Immediately prior to the opening of the new Derby Carriage and Wagon Works in 1876 the Metropolitan Company built twelve of these beautiful Clayton composite carriages for the Scotch expresses. Along with twelve similar vehicles built by the Ashbury Company, they were the first British 12-wheeled carriages and represented the last word in Midland carriage design at the time. They were the predecessors of the standard Clayton round-cornered panelled stock which was, however, non-clerestoried. Running on "American" pattern bogies they were unlike anything previously seen on the Midland and had very high clerestories which almost appeared to be an afterthought. Originally the third class compartments did not have padded seatbacks but they were added later, in 1878. No. 643 was probably scrapped *circa* 1910. *Authors' Collection*

Plate 57. The epitome of Midland passenger comfort. First class dining carriage No. 361 was fitted and decorated by the House of Gillow "regardless of cost" on the Midland's instructions in 1896. It is, therefore, more lavish than the norm, though its companion vehicles were still luxurious, and can be regarded as a PR exercise. *BR*

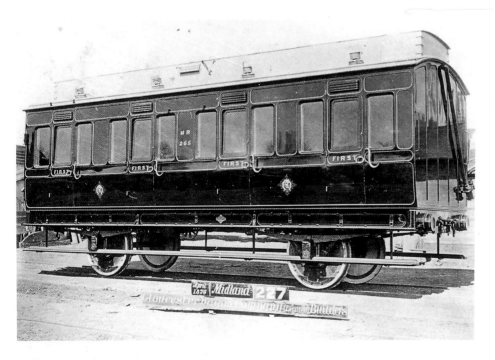

Plate 58. At the opposite end of the spectrum to the magnificent twelve-wheeled clerestory carriages and Pullmans (illustrated later) came the rather humble four and six-wheeled vehicles such as this example. Four-wheeled first No. 265 was built by the Gloucester Wagon Company in 1876 as one of a batch of 25 ordered in 1875 for use on the Moorgate Street–Bedford services. The box on the roof contained a gas bag used to supply the two lamps in each compartment. This apparently precarious arrangement was replaced *circa* 1883 with a tank mounted in the more usual position underneath the floor. Vacuum brakes were fitted at about the same time. Such vehicles would be seen marshalled into trains of between five and twelve carriages for use in the London area well into the LMS era. Four and six-wheeled carriages formed the backbone of the Midland Railway's stock for many years until bogie carriages were introduced in 1875 initially for main line use but later for the more mundane but nevertheless important suburban and secondary routes as well. *Gloucester Railway Carriage & Wagon Co.*

Plate 59. (right) As well as travelling by rail or sea, passengers had to get to and from their stations. Private carriages, taxis and omnibuses were the usual modes of transport, supplemented by Shanks's pony. Between St. Pancras, Charing Cross and Waterloo, however, an omnibus service conveyed passengers holding through tickets to stations on the Midland, South Eastern or London & South Western free of charge (others paid 3d) and the Midland operated omnibuses in London, Manchester, Liverpool and Glasgow. Also at the larger stations various vehicles such as brakes, landaus, broughams and dog carts could be hired, such as this four seater dogcart common in the days before motor transport. *Authors' Collection*

Plate 60. (above) Non-wheeled vehicles also featured in the Midland's inventory, the company possessing quite a large fleet of steamships. The *Duchess of Devonshire* seen here leaving Heysham harbour *circa* 1910 was 1200 tons gross and could steam at 19 knots. She was used on the Heysham–Belfast run. *M.L. Knighton Collection*

Plate 61. (right) Another of the Heysham–Belfast vessels was the TSS *Antrim II* built at the John Brown shipyard in 1904. As this view shows, the dining saloon was well up to the Midland's standards. If the cuisine was as good as the appointments, a journey from London to Belfast on the Midland Railway must have been a *tour gastronomique*. The *Antrim II* was sold to the Isle of Man Steam Packet Company in 1928.
M.L. Knighton Collection

ROYAL TRAINS

At the top of the passenger list, of course, came Royalty, though very few references have been made to Midland Royal travel. The Midland never possessed a purpose built Royal train but did manage to provide a very creditable substitute by refitting standard vehicles and building a Royal saloon. This vehicle was designed by David Bain and built to lot 745 (D.597A) in 1910, the year of King George V's accession, and consisted of a saloon compartment, boudoir, smoking room and attendant's compartment. With the exception of the latter, the coach was panelled and decorated by Messrs. Waring and Gillow Ltd. It was frequently used by the Royal family until 1923; its last Royal use was following the Duke and Duchess of Gloucester's wedding. After this it was demoted to semi-Royal status when the LNWR Royal train became that of the LMS. Fortunately it has survived and been beautifully restored to its former glory by the Midland Railway Trust at whose Butterley centre it can be seen today.

Plate 62. A posed photograph of the Midland Royal train headed by '483' class 4–4–0 No. 504 in June 1921. The locomotive is seen fitted for oil burning as a result of the miners' strike of that year. The train consists of only five vehicles, the 45 ft. brake seen in plate 63 not being present and the 54 ft. first having been remarshalled to the front of the train. *BR*

Plate 63. This train was first used in July 1912 to convey King George V and Queen Mary back to London after a visit to Yorkshire. It comprised 54 ft.brake 1st No. 2782 built to lot 615 of 1905 (D.576), the previously described Royal saloon, 60 ft.1st class dining saloon No. 2754 built to lot 365 of 1895 (D.441), 50 ft. equerries' saloon (altered from a family carriage built in 1909 to lot 664 D.542), 54 ft. 1st No. 2673 built to lot 761 of 1911 (D.600) and 45 ft. brake No. 252 built to lot 675 of 1907 (D.356). The locomotive is 4-4-0 No. 502 of Fowler's '483' class, seemingly commonly used as Royal-train engines (see also Plate 1). *National Railway Museum*

MOTOR TRAINS AND SUCH

Some railways made extensive use of motor trains and their like, but the Midland was not one of them. Small branch lines were their effective homes and, as previously discussed, the Midland had relatively few.

Only four specialised branch train types were tried and there were only ever 16 trains all told. The first were two steam railmotors put into service between Morecambe and Heysham in 1904. They were joint efforts between the locomotive and carriage departments consisting of 60 ft. carriage bodies having an enclosed vertical-boilered steam engine at one end. The boilers were bolted to the leading bogie frames to which were also mounted outside cylinders and Walschaerts valve gear, the whole unit being fixed to the carriage body in a similar manner to the system used on the Great Western. The rear bogie was a standard Midland 8 ft. type. The body was divided into four sections – the engine and driving compartment, luggage compartment, the main saloon accommodating 56 passengers, and a driving vestibule. The two railmotors were numbered 2233 and 2234 in the carriage stock, but M1 and M2 in the locomotive lists. A 43 ft. long non-powered trailer, numbered 2235, was also built but was not fitted with a driving compartment

so the railmotor always had to run around it before the return journey. The next trial was with Pullman drawing room cars Nos. 1, 2, 5 and 10 which were converted for auto train use in accordance with a directive issued on 21st December 1905. They were coupled with 4–4–0 tank engines Nos 8, 10, 19 and 40 borrowed from the Midland and Great Northern Railway and went into service in 1906 on the Wirksworth, Ripley and Melbourne to Derby services as well as the Hemel Hempstead branch. They were discontinued in 1912.

In 1908 seven push-pull sets were assembled consisting of two carriages, modified with driving compartments, sandwiching an 0–4–4 or 0–6–0 tank engine with suitable control gear fitted. Quite a number of locomotives were modified, though it is probable that most were so altered by the LMS which used such trains much more extensively.

Also in 1908 the Lancaster–Morecambe–Heysham line was electrified on the 6.5 kV, 25 Hz single phase overhead system. Three electrically powered cars were built, Nos. 2237 and 2238 having electrical control and bow collectors whilst No. 2236 had Westinghouse control gear and pantographs. Four trailer coaches were also built and the system lasted until early BR days.

Plate 64. The power bogie and boiler of No. 2233 outside Derby Locomotive Works. *BR*

Plate 65. One of the two Midland steam railmotors taking water at Hellifield in 1904 whilst on its way to the Lancaster–Morecambe–Heysham line. The folding step and support brackets fitted over the left hand buffer can be seen clearly. The photograph also shows a standard Midland water crane to advantage, including the two tone colour scheme which was brown and cream. *National Railway Museum*

Plate 66. This picture, taken at Leeds Loco. Junction the same day, shows the non-powered end of the railmotor. Note the difference in cross section between the end portions and the main passenger saloon, a not uncommon feature of David Bain's designs. *National Railway Museum*

New Motor Train, bound for Heysham Harbour.

Plate 67. A postcard, presumably issued in 1905 since the passengers' dress does not appear to indicate the winter of 1904, showing one of the steam railmotors at Morecambe Promenade. The postcard's title is incorrect as in Midland parlance a "Motor Train" consisted of a locomotive and carriages working push–pull. The title should read "New Motor Carriage....." *Authors' Collection*

Plate 68. The interior of Steam Railmotor No. 2233 showing the perforated sycamore seats, gas lamps and interior projections of the torpedo vents. The carriage was wood panelled and highly varnished. *BR*

Plate 69. In 1917 No. 2234 was converted into a Superintendent's saloon and was teamed with Johnson single No. 600 which was concurrently fitted with a Deeley cab vacuum control gear. This photograph was taken after the grouping but before September 1928 when No. 600 was withdrawn. *Authors' Collection*

Plate 70. M & GN 4–4–0T No. 8 and ex Pullman Parlour Car No. 10 converted for motor train working. The locomotive was built by Hudswell, Clark & Rogers for the Yarmouth & North Norfolk Railway in 1879, whilst the Pullman car originally entered services in January 1877 named *Apollo*. By October 1906 the locomotive had been renumbered 2 and coupled to car No. 2, so this photograph must have been taken earlier in 1906. No detailed drawings of the locomotives or carriage conversions are thought to survive, but the locomotives are known to have received Deeley smokeboxes and chimneys later. *Authors' Collection*

Plate 71. One of the few Midland push-pull sets consisting of 48 ft. brake third No. 0500, '1102' class 0–6–0 tank No. 1632 and 48 ft. brake composite No. 3567, all modified in 1908 for driving from the outer carriage ends. *R.J. Essery Collection*

Plate 72. A three car electric train on the Lancaster–Morecambe–Heysham line in May 1908. The power car, No. 2237, was one of two with electrical control gear and bow collectors. The leading and rear trailers are Nos. 2240 and 2242. *J. Turnbull Collection*

Plate 73. **(left)** A close-up view of the vacuum control gear fitted to No.1632. *BR*

HANDLING THE FREIGHT

Like many other British railways, the Midland derived a large proportion of its revenue from goods and mineral traffic. By 1922 it owned more goods vehicles than any other British company – a colossal 115 349 of them. A great deal of this traffic was coal emanating from the rich coalfields of Derbyshire, Nottinghamshire and parts of Yorkshire where many collieries had direct rail connections with Midland lines. One of the most common sights on the system was a huge coal train between Toton and Cricklewood, made up of Midland and privately-owned wagons from either collieries or coal merchants, rumbling south.

The frequency of these trains is illustrated by the fact that special goods lines and a costly tunnel were built to avoid Sharnbrook summit between Irchester and Bedford.

The vast majority of Midland wagons were simple open types. Only slightly more than 10% were covered wagons and there were relatively few specialist vehicles. Prior to the opening of the new Carriage and Wagon Works at Derby in 1876 many items of goods stock were built by outside contractors and little standardisation would have been evident. The appointment of Thomas Gethin Clayton as Carriage and Wagon Superintendent in 1873 heralded a new era in wagon as well as coaching stock policy and much scrapping and rebuilding took place. From 1882, in an attempt to rid the system of large numbers of second rate private owner wagons, the Midland purchased large numbers of them which were scrapped or rebuilt. It is out of place here to go much further into the history of Midland wagon development as there are excellent books available on the subject such as "Midland Wagons Volumes I and II" by Bob Essery published by OPC. As well as Midland and privately-owned wagons, those belonging to other railway companies also found their way into the Midland system, particularly after 1916 when Derby entered into a common user agreement whereby goods wagons from many companies were used as common stock.

The handling of all this traffic was one of the Company's major undertakings and, in the days before long distance road transport, the vast majority of stations across the system had goods facilities of one sort or another. Some had only small yards to handle local traffic, such as Idridgehay on the Wirksworth branch with its cattle dock and siding space. At the other end of the scale was the huge Somers Town Goods Depot adjacent to St. Pancras, built to handle enormous quantities of all types of goods coming into London. There were also specialised locations such as Toton marshalling yards and the St. Pancras beer vaults to which reference is made later. At smaller yards there may have been a goods shed and hand crane for handling loads whereas large depots were often equipped with several sheds and warehouses, hydraulic lifts for goods or even whole wagons, and large numbers of horse-drawn, or later mechanically-powered, road vehicles. There were also docks, canal wharves and barges, ships, storage tanks and a host of other aspects to handling the freight and we can only illustrate a small part of the whole. The subject is a fascinating one and to misquote Essery & Rowlands, "To those for whom the clash of loose coupled wagons is music, this section is dedicated".

Plate 74. A superb assortment of Midland and private owner wagons at Wigston Junction yards on 20th March 1905. The yards were located to the south of Leicester adjacent to the triangular junction of the Birmingham and London routes and a wide variety of loads are in evidence though coal and mineral wagons predominate. Some of the private owner vehicles are from concerns well known on the Midland such as Nunn, Cornwall and Rother Vale. The brake van towards the right of the scene is in ex-works condition with very light grey finish and white roof and makes a striking contrast with much darker on by the locomotive shed in the background. The shed itself was a standard Midland roundhouse. Note the huge, shaped coal stack in front of it. *BR*

Plate 75. The Midland was above all a coal carrier, taking the products of the rich Nottinghamshire, Derbyshire and South Yorkshire coalfields to London. This view of Cricklewood Sidings in March 1903 gives some indication of the volume of traffic which was handled. Private owner wagons predominate, interspersed with the Midland's own vehicles. Note the vast difference in clarity of the wagon letters "MR" despite the use of supposedly self cleaning oxalic paint. The rural surroundings of both Wigston and Cricklewood contrast sharply with the scenes today. *BR*

Plate 76. The northern end of the Midland's coal trail to London on 14th February 1910. Situated at the end of the Erewash Valley line between Nottingham and Derby, the massive Toton marshalling yards were the assembly point for wagons from the Midlands and South Yorkshire pits before their journey to London. A large number of shunters was employed at Toton sorting and assembling trains, and accidents became so regular that in 1895 the company built a special brake van for carrying seriously injured men from the yards. Known as an "ambulance van" it was looked after by a railway ambulance team. *BR*

Plate 77. The famous crooked spire identifies the location of this photograph, taken on 5th July 1911, as Chesterfield. It shows straight framed '240' class Kirtley 0-6-0 No. 2300 (built in August 1850 as No. 240) at the head of a Toton–Cricklewood coal train having just passed under the bridge carrying the Great Central line from Lincoln. The leading wagons belong to Stephenson Clarke & Co, one of the largest concerns regularly involved in shipping coal to London. *BR*

Plate 78. Birmingham Central Goods Yard on 22nd September 1922 gives some indication of the extent of Midland goods traffic in the last year of its independent existence. Wagons from at least eight "foreign" companies are in evidence as well as the Caledonian Railway tarpaulin sheet in the foreground. Not how the timber loads are lashed into the open wagons. *R.J. Essery Collection*

Plate 79. Nedham Street Sidings, Leicester, on 14th April 1922. Located just north of the main LNWR and MR Leicester goods depots, these sidings were equipped with an overhead crane, seen on the right of the picture, for handling heavy loads. *BR*

Plate 80. Big town and city goods depots required a great deal of administrative effort. This photograph, taken on 15th May 1922, shows the substantial Ancoats goods offices and, in the background, the large MR grain warehouse. The picture also shows the appearance of the Company's draymen and their horses and vehicles. The unattached, or trace, horses were the equine equivalent of the banking engines used to assist heavy loads on hills. *R.J. Essery Collection*

Plate 81. The Midland's goods and receiving warehouse in Liverpool's Victoria Street also served as goods offices and passenger parcels centre. Although the Midland did not enter Liverpool on its own tracks, it ran into two of the city's three main line stations via the CLC and L & YR, and had its own locomotive sheds and goods facilities. That its Victoria Street site was a busy one is evidenced in this view which also shows that the Midland took no chance of the passer-by being unaware of its ownership! *BR*

Plate 82. An interesting assortment of wagons at Nottingham on 27th March 1922 with the passenger station in the background. Apart from the wagons and their loads, the picture has many points of interest such as the Acfield steel signal arms, bracket signal arms, bracket signal detail and wooden covering for the point rodding. Note also the fogman's hut and braziers and the fact that the distant arms still have horizontal stripes on their faces at this late date. *BR*

Plate 83. Nottingham Wilford Road yard on 31st March 1922. Several of the wagons are covered with tarpaulin sheets which was common practice at the time. The Midland sheet stores were at nearby Trent. Wilford Road also had a travelling crane and was used by local coal merchants whose small tip carts are in the foreground. *National Railway Museum*

Plate 84. Typical of the goods facilities provided at smaller suburban and country stations were those at Bulwell just north of Nottingham on the line to Kirkby-in-Ashfield. As this view taken on 3rd April 1922 shows, even such a small yard enjoyed plenty of business. *BR*

Plate 85. On the same day this evocative photograph of Radford goods yard was taken. It illustrates well the substantially built goods shed, most of which on the Midland were long lived brick or stone structures, and the standard heavy yard crane. The stone steps leading to the goods office bear testimony to the amount of business concluded there. *BR*

Plate 86. Of the Midland's vast wagon fleet no less than 63 000 were five-plank high sided goods wagons built to D.299. This publicity photograph, provisionally dated during the 1890s, shows a rake of them outside Ley's Foundry which still stands close to Derby Midland station. Although all supposedly painted the same there was a vast difference between wagons once they had been in service a while as graphically illustrated by the two right hand vehicles. Towards the left hand end are some private owner wagons and an old dumb buffered wagon. *R.C. Betts Collection*

Plate 87. Apart from legions of open or covered goods wagons and other common types, there were specialised vehicles too. Many of them were attached to passenger trains or were marshalled into trains which ran at express speeds because of the perishable nature of their contents, and these vehicles were often classified as non passenger coaching stock. Such a vehicle was this ventilated milk van seen at Cinderford on the Severn & Wye joint *circa* 1910. The roof profile and round cornered beading are obvious coaching stock features.
Authors' Collection

Plate 88. Another location on the Midland system was Luton–centre of the millinery industry. In this 1905 view of Luton goods yard large numbers of hat boxes are being transferred from goods drays into D.299 open wagons. Once the boxes were stacked in the wagons and securely lashed in place they were sheeted over.
J. Turnbull Collection

Plate 89. The large numbers of horses employed on the Midland all needed feeding and in 1902 the Company built a provender depot, just north of Oakham station near to Langham Signal Box, to supply their needs. This view was taken in June 1906 from the roof of the provender stores and shows the associated sidings. By 1910 the depot had gained the reputation of being one of the finest anywhere and was supplying feed for some 4000 horses. Special feed was supplied to Heysham for feeding Irish racehorses in transit. The store remained in railway use until 1954 when it was taken over by a firm of seed merchants.
R.C. Betts Collection

Plate 90. The Midland Railway's goods catchment area included the country's industrial heartland where it had to deal with some very large and awkward loads. Many types of special wagon were built for such traffic, some of which are seen here on 9th December 1906 carrying a heavy naval gun at Toton. On the right of the picture is a D.333 traction wagon, whilst the gun barrel is shackled to two D.328 armour plate wagons. *National Railway Museum*

Plate 91. Around 1922 Messrs. John and Edwin Wright of Birmingham asked the Midland to transport a 36 300 foot long flattened strand wire rope weighing 65 tons. Two D.340 bogie rail wagons were modified for the task and this view shows them receiving their load. *BR*

Plate 92. Like town and city goods depots, docks were important and busy centres of the Midland's freight handling activities. This view of Bristol Avon Street wharf was taken on 30th May 1922 and shows Midland and other companies' wagons, dockside cranes, road vehicles and barges all mutually engaged in freight distribution. Two of the barges are Nos. 6 & 18 of the Midland Railway's own fleet. *BR*

Plate 93. Another Sheffield location on 13th May 1912 – this time Queens Road Yard. On the left of the picture is the stables and in front of them a weighbridge hut. The brilliantly white cattle dock appears to have been drawn on the negative for some reason. Note the point levers and the trap points in the foreground. This photograph is taken from the bridge at Charlotte Road, from where one of your publishers first gained an interest in railways as a small boy. *National Railway Museum*

Plate 94. Sheffield Wicker Goods Depot on 13th May 1912. The photograph was taken from the overhead travelling crane, the rails for which can be seen either side of the "junk pile" in the foreground, some of which is scrap iron for the steelworks. Some specialised vehicles are in evidence such as the 16 ft. 6 in. long banana van on the right (next to the H & BR wagon) and many different types of horse drawn vehicles are present including drays and a timber wagon. *BR*

Plate 95. One of the Heysham Harbour tug/tenders, appropriately named *Wyvern*, as seen on 9th April 1908 in front of the long quay and a rake of at least 30 open wagons. The vessel was built by Ferguson Bros. of Part Glasgow in 1905 and had a long and illustrious career, not being withdrawn until June 1960. *J. Turnbull Collection*

· MIDLAND RAILWAY · HEYSHAM HARBOUR ·

DEPTH OF WATER in the harbour 17 ft., and 40 ft. outside entrance, at low water ordinary Spring tides.

LANDING FACILITIES at all states of the tide.

QUAY LENGTH 3000 ft.

ELECTRIC LIFTS & TRAVELLING CRANES and electric light in the Passenger Station, Goods Sheds and Harbour.

HORSES, CATTLE & OTHER LIVE STOCK are landed on sloping ways & without slings. Extensive accommodation for resting & grazing.

LARGE AREA FOR STORAGE of timber, pig iron, slates & other traffic not requiring cover.

FISH STAGE for unloading fish from trawlers or smacks with covered accommodation for packing, sorting, &c. Facilities for storing ice, coaling or ballasting vessels, etc.

TRAINS ARRIVE & DEPART ALONGSIDE STEAMERS.

ENQUIRIES for berths & all information may be addressed to:—
Captain Beasley, Harbour Master & Traffic Agent, Heysham.
Messrs. Little & Co., Heysham, Barrow & Albert Sq., Belfast.
or the Chief Goods Manager or General Superintendent, Derby.

W. Guy Granet, General Manager.

M. Secretan.

Plate 96. As previously described, the Midland's Irish traffic grew to the extent that the Company built a complete harbour complex at Heysham. As this publicity poster dated 5th December 1910 shows, extensive goods handling facilities were provided. The inset map indicates that regular sailings took place to and from Belfast, Londonderry, Dublin and Douglas (I.O.M.) *J. Turnbull Collection*

Plate 97. Up to the early years of twentieth century even goods trains were hauled by fully lined locomotives as this photograph of Kirtley '480' class 0–6–0 No. 596 with a train of open wagons shows. Seen near Bentham on the "little" North Western line *circa* 1903 the engine was built by Kitson & Co. in 1867 and withdrawn in 1928. It was fitted with a Johnson boiler and fittings in 1881 and sports a built up chimney. *Authors' Collection*

Plate 98. Despite the preponderance of D.299s, Midland goods trains could display a wide variety of wagons. This wonderfully mixed goods passing Kings Norton on 16th July 1921 illustrates the point. Note that the cattle wagons are marshalled near the front of the train. *W.L. Good*

Plate 99. In May 1879 the Traffic Committee ordered a bullion van for the London to Liverpool gold shipments destined for foreign parts. The van, No. 60, was 21 ft. long and weighed 10½ tons, some 3½ tons more than a parcels van of comparable size. This extra weight was due to the strengthened bullion room, the door to which is behind the open double doors; it was lit by four rooflights, two of which can be seen above the rainstrip and which delineate the room's size. Next to the bullion room was a guard's compartment. The van was replaced in 1912 by one of the two LT & S bullion vans Nos. 1 & 2 taken into Midland stock and renumbered 60 and 127 in the Post Office series.
P.R. Bunce Collection

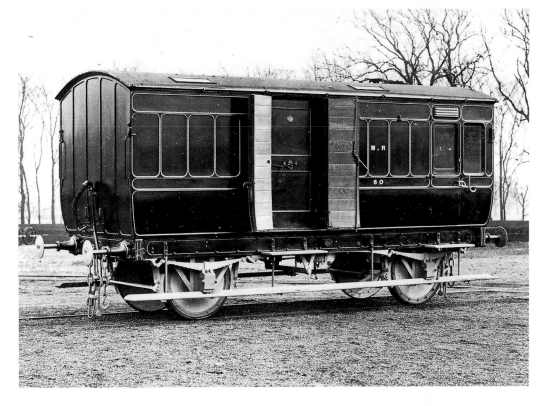

Plate 100. A goods train on the "Long Drag" near Ribblehead *circa* 1910. The front portion of the train is made up of D.299 wagons which appear to be empty, though the variations in height suggest that some may be loaded. The locomotive is No. 3002 built by Neilson's in 1876 and which lasted until 1960. *Authors' Collection*

Plate 101. The Midland was renowned for double heading trains over many of its routes. This mineral train on the London extension *circa* 1920 is powered by Armstrong Whitworth 4F No. 3869 and an unidentified '700' class 0–6–0. Judging by the exhausts, the Kirtley is either more efficiently fired than the 4F or is letting its younger colleague do the lion's share of the work. *R. Carpenter Collection*

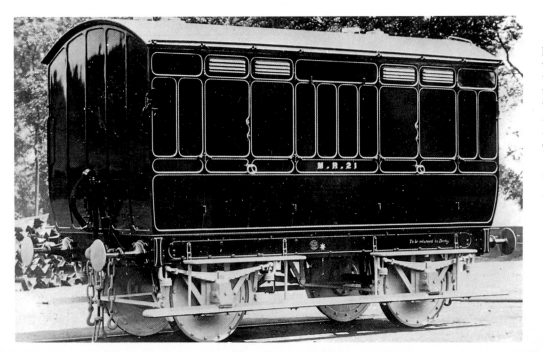

Plate 102. One of the less advertised and more macabre types of traffic with which the Railway had to cope was corpses. Four corpse vans were built in 1888 to lot 199 and once again the roof profile and panelling are obviously those of coaching stock. As with plate 105 the underframe and running gear details are clearly visible. The legend at the right hand end of the solebar reads, "To be returned to Derby". There were two lockable "compartments" – the locks can be seen above the waist panelling on the vertical beading. The guidees for the communication cord can be seen along the edge of the roof.
A. Brown Collection

Plate 103. Midland and North Eastern Joint Postal Stock sorting van No. 14. Built in 1879 for the Midland's own use it was transferred to the M & NEJPS when the service started in 1889, and replaced in the Midland lists with new 43 ft.stock. This photograph was taken in the 1890s (note the monogram above the red painted late fee letterbox) and shows both the sorting staff and the traductor arms loaded with mailbags. These bags would be picked up by lineside apparatus whilst the train maintained running speed; similarly the net would collect mail for sorting. Other points to note include the "Lansdowne" gangway on one end only and the coupling safety chains connected. Originally built with oil lighting it is seen here as subsequently gas lit. *By courtesy of the Post Office*

Plate 104. The Midland also made provision for theatrical companies and the like. In 1920/21 it built four theatrical scenery vans on secondhand 44 ft. 10 in. underframes to lot 950. No. 674 shows its ornate lining which accentuates the outside framing. Not the large side and end doors for loading "flats". *Authors' Collection*

Plate 105. One of the more perishable commodities carried was fish and this picture shows one of the earliest special fish trucks dating from 1887. The ensemble consists simply of a large fish box, in this case No. 17, on what more or less amounts to an open carriage truck No. 121. The Midland lot book records 48 of these vehicles being built and as can be seen in the photograph the wagons and boxes were fully lined out. The running gear appears to be painted in photographic grey which allows us to see detail which would otherwise be hidden. *BR*

Plate 106. At the other end of the scale was the final design of MR fish van. This particular example was one of 20 built at Derby in 1920 to lot 947. Another 20 were ordered in 1922 but were not actually built until after the grouping. *Authors' Collection*

Plate 107 As seen in plate 81 parcels and luggage were part of the freight handling process. Such items were often carried in 6-wheeled full brake carriages such as No. 29 seen here in pristine condition. First introduced in 1897 for the Bristol to Bradford expresses, they were soon adopted for general use and, by 1901, five batches totalling 301 vehicles had been built. The first 63 were 13 ft. 3 in. high and the remainder 13 ft. 1 in. high, 30 were built for Midland and Scottish joint stock in 1898 with gangways. When first built they had a much larger guard's lookout, but following an accident in 1899 they were removed and the smaller type seen in this photograph were fitted. Between removal and refitting some vehicles ran for a time without any lookouts at all. All survived well into the post grouping period, some even into BR days, and eight of the joint stock examples passed into LNER ownership. The slate coloured panels in the waist were for chalking destinations and other information about the consignments carried. *BR*

Plate 108. As well as moving freight by rail, the Company had to transport it to and from its stations or yards. In 1890 it owned about 3000 road vehicles, all built by outside contractors to an almost equally large number of designs. From this time, however, the Midland appointed Mr. Fred Crocker to supervise the building of a range of standard vehicles. One example was this 10 ton timber truck with adjustable rear bolster, timber supports and clamps for poles. *Authors' Collection*

Plate 109. A larger version of the timber truck – this one having a capacity of 15 tons – with iron wheels and heavier central beam. These vehicles were built for a single horse between the shafts; assistance on hills could be given by trace horses such as those seen in plate 80. *Authors' Collection*

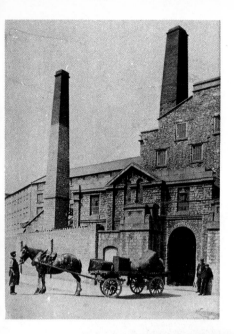

Plate 110. (left) A standard Midland goods dray at Carr's Mill, Twerton, Bath. Although of relatively poor quality, this *circa* 1910 view has been included to show how carefully the vehicle was loaded! *C.G. Maggs Collection*

Plate 111. (right) With the large number of horses employed there was a need or taking care of sick or injured animals. To transport them to horse hospitals these two wheeled floats were used. They were reversible vehicles with moveable shafts and doors at both ends, and the bodies were very low slung necessitating a cranked axle. *R.J. Essery Collection*

Plate 112. There were also 195 mechanically and electrically powered vehicles in MR ownership at the end of 1922. From the early 1900s petrol and steam driven lorries were purchased and from 1916 some battery powered vehicles were acquired. This Straker 5 ton steam lorry was built in 1904 and as can be seen was restricted to 5 m.p.h. Judging by the solid tyres and primitive suspension this would appear to have been a wise move! The lorry is standing on a wagon turntable which is flush timbered, the fixed rails in the picture also being set into the surface. This was originally for the benefit of shunting horses so that they would not trap their hooves or otherwise injure themselves. The practice was also carried into many sidings for the same reason. *R.J. Essery Collection*

MIDLAND RAILWAY
COLLECTING VAN
FOR
GOODS & PARCELS.
MIDLAND RAILWAY. St PANCRAS
565

Plate 113. For smaller goods consignments and parcels the Midland built 1 ton covered parcels vans such as No. 565 seen here at St. Pancras. The panel at the rear of the van was for posters, timetables etc. Some Midland vehicles became standard LMS types and this was one of them. *R.J. Essery Collection*

Plate 114. This view of Birmingham Central goods depot on 1st July 1895 shows some of the vast numbers of men and the large patient railway horses which were used for handling the freight. By the time of the grouping the Midland Railway possessed 7066 horse drawn vehicles. *BR*

AMERICAN MIDLAND

The history of American equipment on the Midland dates from before the Company's formation. In 1839 the Birmingham & Gloucester Railway started buying locomotives from William Norris of Philadelphia. The reasons for this are complex and beyond our present scope. Suffice it to say that locomotives were needed for, amongst other things, climbing the notorious 1 in 37 Lickey incline and although English firms such as R. Stephenson & Co. could have built acceptable types, it would appear that they declined even to quote for the job. Of the locomotives available "off the shelf" the Norris 4–2–0 was almost certainly the most suitable single driver type for gradients and Capt. W.S. Moorsom, then engineer of the line, decided on their adoption.

The Birmingham & Gloucester eventually possessed 26 of the type including nine built by the English firms of B. Hick & Sons (who built 3) and Nasmyth Gaskell & Co. The first was delivered from America in March 1839 and the last in May 1842. Fifteen lasted long enough to receive Midland numbers and the last example was withdrawn in 1856. They are commonly associated with two things; firstly their work on the Lickey incline which they performed outstandingly well (though they also did much general work on the rest of the line), and secondly the accident at Bromsgrove in November 1840 when two men were killed by a boiler explosion. In fact it was not a Norris locomotive which exploded, but a certain Dr. Church's experimental tank engine called Surprise (!). Unfortunately the stonemason carving the deceaseds' headstones took as his model the first locomotive he saw, and that was a Norris 4–2–0. This is verified by newspaper reports and contemporary records. One of the American engines was involved in a fatal accident in April 1841 when it blew out a tube plug and killed the Company's locomotive superintendent, Mr. Crewze, who was driving it.

THE PULLMAN CARS. In 1872 the Midland's General Manager James (late Sir James) Allport toured the U.S.A. and was much impressed with the luxury of travel. On his return he persuaded the Board of Directors to invite George Pullman to meet them and explain how American railroads ran trains which included his elegant coaches. They were impressed and recommended that the Midland did likewise. The outcome was the introduction of Pullman coaches into the Midland in 1874.

The vehicles were sent from the Pullman works at Detroit as a kit of parts which were assembled in purpose built sheds at Derby. Initially there were two types, the 'drawing room' or 'parlour' car and the convertible sleeping car. The former was basically an open saloon with two rows of comfortable swivelling armchairs down the sides whilst the sleeper had plush bench type seats with tables between. In theory, therefore, they could be used as diners though no kitchen was provided. In sleeper mode the tables were lowered to form double beds, and bunks were hinged down from the ceiling. Curtains could be drawn to separate the vehicle into small compartments where passengers could undress in privacy, even though they had to sit on the bed to do so. This could not have been easy for the ladies with their bulky and elaborate costumes!

At first the coaches were owned by the Pullman company who collected a supplementary fee from passengers riding in them after they had paid the normal first class fare to the Midland. Later the Midland bought them and changed the names for numbers. The parlour cars were not very popular with the travelling public and the Midland rebuilt some of the Pullmans into picnic saloons and the like; as such hey remained in use until soon after the turn of the century. As previously described, four were used from 1905 to 1912 as push–pull units, and many lasted until quite recently with the bogies removed as mess huts, etc.

In 1900 four more sleeping cars were obtained from the Pullman company though the Midland provided the underframes and running gear. Three of them lasted into LMS days and, as can be seen in plate 116, they were of more conventional lines than the earlier vehicles, though still unmistakably Pullman in origin.

THE "YANKEE" MOGULS. During the winter of 1898/9 the Midland urgently needed main line goods locomotives. Derby works was crammed to capacity and outside contractors' order books were full. The situation was not improved by a series of engineering strikes and delivery times stretched to 15 months or more. So the Midland, in company with the Great Northern and Great Central, turned to Burnham, Williams & Co's Baldwin works in Philadelphia. In February 1899 an order was placed for twenty locomotives "equal in power to the (Midland's) standard goods engine". A few weeks later it was decided to order twenty more but the Baldwin works could only supply ten, so the Schenectady Locomotive works in New York state undertook to build the remainder.

Like the Pullmans, the engines were delivered as crates of parts and were assembled at Derby. Fortunately the summer of 1899 was a good one as there was no workshop space for the Baldwins and they had to be erected outdoors. They were basically a standard Baldwin 2–6–0 design and, with bar frames, huge domelike sandboxes on the boilers, high split running plates and smokebox stays, they were very American in appearance. They had 4000 gallon bogie tenders though these were quite different from those built by the Midland for the Compounds, singles and Belpaire 4–4–0s. Numbered 2501–10 and 2521–40 they were built very quickly and the first was in service by the end of May 1899.

In contrast, the Schenectadys were much more Anglicised. They had tapered boilers and smooth reverse curved running plates, though they were also bar framed and had enormous domes. The tenders were almost identical to standard Johnson 3250 gallon ones. All in all they were attractive engines – certainly much more so than the Baldwins.

Both types had features never before seen on the Midland. Most striking were the large side windowed cabs with extended roofs which helped keep the crews dry. Unfortunately the intrusion of over 2 ft. of boiler could also keep them very hot, and the design made little impression on Mr. Johnson who carried on providing his engines with much smaller, draughtier offerings. They had outside cylinders with easily accessible valve ports and glands, which must have made life easier for fitters used to crawling into the cramped space between Midland frames, but despite their good points they were not popular. They were more expensive to run than their British counterparts, using more coal and oil and being costly to maintain. As Johnson pointed out in reply to much criticism in the railway press, however, they were £400 cheaper and, more to the point, they were readily available. In Midland terms they were only short lived and by August 1915 all had gone to the breaker's torch.

Plate 115. Pullman drawing room car No. 13 at Derby *circa* 1884. When built in 1877 it was named Eclipse and carried the legend "Pullman" on the eaves panel where "Midland" appears in this view. Both were changed when the Midland bought it in 1883. *Authors' Collection*

Plate 116. One of the four Pullman sleeping carriages introduced in April 1900 with Midland built underframes and running gear. No. 35 was the only one which did not survive into LMS days, being scrapped shortly before the grouping. *National Railway Museum*

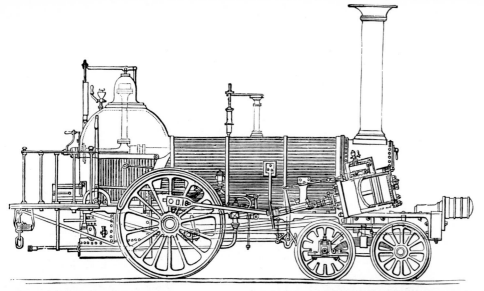

This part sectional elevation of a Norris 4–2–0 is believed to represent *Philadelphia* built in 1840 in the city of that name. The class was known as 'A Extra'. Philadelphia was rebuilt in 1842 as a saddle tank and was withdrawn in 1856. Assuming the drawing to be authentic a number of interesting features are apparent, most noticeably the long wheelbase and steeply inclined cylinder, the centreline of which is not coincident with the wheel centres.

Plate 117. The only photograph we know of showing a "Yankee Mogul" at the head of a train of passenger vehicles, though the headcode indicates an empty stock train. Schenectady 2–6–0 No. 2233 (they were renumbered in 1907) is seen at Birmingham New Street in May 1914. Originally No. 2514 it was withdrawn 15 months later. *W.L. Good*

Plate 118. A Baldwin 2–6–0 being erected outside Derby works in the summer of 1899. The only alterations to the standard American design were the drawhook, buffers and lampirons. *Authors' Collection*

Plate 119. The same locomotive shortly after completion. The large forward "dome" is, in fact, a sandbox. The typically American features referred to in the text can be clearly seen. *Authors' Collection*

Plate 120. A Schenectady Mogul enjoying the comparative luxury of being assembled under cover at Derby in 1899, with one of its brethren in a less advanced state alongside it. The Midland loading gauge made it necessary to cut down the overall width as the flattened sides to the cylinder cladding shows. *Authors' Collection*

ST. PANCRAS

At its incorporation the Midland's only method of getting its passenger and goods traffic to London was to hand them over to the London & Birmingham (which became part of the London & North Western) at Rugby or Hampton in Arden. This state of affairs, however, did not satisfy the ambitions of the Derby boardroom and ways were sought of running Midland trains into the Capital. After Hudson's departure relationships with the Great Northern improved and eventually negotiations were successfully concluded to build a line to a junction with that company's tracks at Hitchin and thence share its route into London and accommodation at King's Cross. The line was completed in 1857 and at once Midland traffic poured south onto what were rapidly becoming the most crowded railway lines in the world. By the mid 1860s congestion on the line and in the station was unbelievable and it was obvious that the only real solution was for the Midland to find its own route and terminus.

Thus was born the London extension of the Midland Railway and work began on St. Pancras Station in 1866, literally over the road from King's Cross. The Midland wanted an imposing presence in London and it got what it wanted at a price. The design was on a magnificent scale and Barlow's train shed had the largest single span roof yet built measuring 245 ft. in width at platform level, 100 ft. in height at the crown and 689 ft. in length. Underlying the entire station were cavernous beer vaults accessed via a wagon lift at the north end of the platforms. in these vaults was stored the vast traffic from Burton on Trent brought by the Midland to quench Southern thirsts – a traffic which had been an important planning consideration when the London extension was conceived. The spacing of the hundreds of pillars passing through the vaults to support the station above had as one of its influencing factors the need to store as many barrels as possible between them and this in turn affected the station's dimensions; thus St. Pancras can be said, without stretching credulity too far, to have been designed around a beer barrel! The vaults also housed the Midland's largest single staff grade (unpaid) – the St. Pancras cats. There is a note in the Minute Books of the company to the effect thay they were introduced deliberately to keep down the mice and rats, a task they have performed admirably since the station opened.

St. Pancras station opened on 1st October 1868 though photographs of the time show it as being still incomplete. Even less complete, however, was the St. Pancras hotel which was not finished until 1876 despite being opened on 5th May 1873 (shades of the Costa Packet!). This imposing building was bought "off the shelf" so to speak as it had been originally designed as a contender for the new Foreign Office by Gilbert Scott; its modification and transplanting to Euston road earned the architect a knighthood. Below the staff quarters in the attic were four floors of rich Victorian luxury and the hotel's reputation soon became second to none.

In June 1892 the storage roads in the station were replaced by another pair of platforms (today's platforms 3 & 4) to provide more passenger room; this was the only major alteration the Midland ever made to the station apart from signalling. The old signal boxes (plate 47) were replaced in the early 1900s by a huge 80 ft. box at the junction of the lines to Somers Town goods depot (built in the 1880s to the west of the station) and two boxes placed back to back in the station throat (See plate 216). The other major signalling modification was Acfield's replacement in June 1914 of the original 42 arms and 21 dolls of the main signal gantry with 16 arms, 8 dolls and mechanical route indicators. It was in this condition that St. Pancras passed into the ownership of the London, Midland & Scottish Railway....

Plate 121. This postcard *circa* 1910 is included primarily because it shows a passenger's eye view of the interior of St. Pancras. Most contemporary panoramic views were taken from loftier positions. *Authors' Collection*

Plate 122. A view showing Scott's St. Pancras hotel and Somers Town Goods station. The scene now is considerably altered – the goods station having been more or less flattened and the buildings in the right foreground replaced by offices. The signboard to the right of the goods station entrance advertises a "wholesale depot for potatoes and general produce", whilst a series of posters adorns the verticals between the window arches. The traffic on Euston Road appears quite heavy for May 1922; one wonders how the roadsweeper would fare today! *BR*

Plate 123. The ubiquitous 0–4–4 tanks took charge of much suburban traffic out of St. Pancras. No. 2626, renumbered 1426 in 1907, is ready to depart *circa* 1905 with such a train. Built in 1900 she passed into LMS, and later BR, hands and was not scrapped until 1953. *Authors' Collection*

Plate 124. The presence of the signal box on Platform 1, described in plate 126, dates this fine view of St. Pancras train shed as pre-1876. The picture contains a wealth of early London extension detail. Some points worth noting are the early pattern ground signals, four and six wheeled oil lit carriages with roof luggage racks, horse boxes and carriage trucks near the camera. The overall neatness and cleanliness is notable – especially the screen and roof glazing. *National Railway Museum*

Plate 125. The famous actress Sarah Bernhardt and her entourage about to board a train at St. Pancras on 28th July 1894. An unsubstantiated rumour, but one the authors are happy to spread, is that Miss Bernhardt always insisted on travelling with the Midland if her journey permitted it. The vehicle she is about to board appears to be a Clayton saloon to lot 7 of 1877. *National Railway Museum*

Plate 126. The first signalboxes at St. Pancras were small structures situated on what became platforms 1 and 6. This photograph shows the former and is provisionally dated between January 1869, when installation of gas lighting commenced, and September of that year when it was completed. The pristine condition of the box also suggest newness. *National Railway Museum*

OTHER STATIONS

Just as there is an image of a typical Midland passenger train, so also is there a picture of a typical Midland station, or to be exact two typical Midland stations – St. Pancras and the others! The "typical" Midland country station has diagonal sawn paling fences, stone building and glazed sawtooth platform canopies. There is also a crossover, stone built goods shed and end loading bay whilst passengers cross from one platform to the other via an iron lattice footbridge. There were stations like that on the Midland, but in a system as diverse in origin, geography and chronology it is hardly surprising that there was, in fact, a wide variety of architectural styles, layouts and details. The subject would require a great deal of space to do it justice and the major work to date is by V.R. Anderson and G.K. Fox entitled "A Pictorial Record of Midland Railway Architecture" (OPC 1985). In these pages we would merely like to give some idea of the widely differing types of station at which a passenger on the Midland may have found himself.

Plate 127. Spondon station about 3 miles south of Derby on the old Midland Counties line *circa* 1910. Note the style of fencing ont the left of the picture and the rural surroundings. *D.J. White Collection*

Plate 128. The entrance and booking hall of Water Orton station situated on the road bridge over the platforms as seen in December 1908. Note that there are no apparent signs of ownership.
M.L. Knighton Collection

Plate 129. One of an official series of views of the interior of the newly opened station at Morecambe Promenade on 24th March 1907, built to replace the older, somewhat cramped, station at Northumberland Street.
BR

Plate 130. Broom Junction *circa* 1910. The Evesham & Redditch Railway of the Midland, opened to freight on the 16th June 1866 and to passenger traffic on 17th September of that year. Broom Junction came into being as a result of the desire of the East & West Junction Railway to extend its interests west of Stratford under the Evesham, Redditch and Stratford–on–Avon Railway Act of 5th August 1873. When opened on 2nd June 1879, the station was solely an exchange platform between the two lines, a role which it retained until November 1880. This view north from a road overbridge shows the station at the time it was controlled by two signalboxes, north and south. The signal to the right of the bracket was for the Stratford line, whilst that to the left indicated route clearance or otherwise for the Evesham direction. *R.C. Betts Collection*

Plate 131. A fine view of Leicester (London Road) station in 1897. The locomotive at Platform 2 is one of Kirtley's '890' class 2–4–0s rebuilt by Johnson. The trap points at the end of the locomotive release road appear to have served their purpose at sometime judging by the condition of the wooden wedges at the ends of the rails. The cleanliness and tidiness of the station speaks of an era when staff economies were unknown. *National Railway Museum*

Plate 132. Wombwell, just south of Barnsley, was well equipped with railway stations. The Midland station, seen here in the winter of 1910, was not far from the Great Central station of the same name. The obvious potential for confusion was removed by naming them Wombwell West and Wombwell Central respectively – in 1950! In 1964 Central closed and the Midland station became plain Wombwell once more in 1969. *Authors' Collection*

Plate 133. The delightful station at Ripple between Tewkesbury and Malvern Wells in the early years of the present century. Note the differing roof profiles, platform edging and vertical sawn fencing. *Authors' Collection*

Plate 134. The branch from Ashchurch, on the Birmingham and Gloucester line, to Broom Junction and Barnt Green was opened in stages. The rather plain looking station at Alvechurch was on the Redditch Railway portion opened in 1859. The bay window on the platform side of the station master's house is unusual. *Authors' Collection*

Plate 135. Even on the "standardised" Settle & Carlisle line, Culgaith station was an exception. The station buildings were the only ones not built to one of the normal variatons on a theme as illustrated in the many books written about the line.
R.C. Betts Collection

Plate 136. A large Settle & Carlisle station, unusual in having an island platform on the right with a large canopy. This view of Hawes Junction, later Garsdale, looking north was probably taken *circa 1900. J.H. Wright courtesy K.C. Woodhead*

Plate 137. The lesser known Clapham junction where the Ingleton branch left the Lancaster & Morecambe line from Skipton. The station was built by the "little" North Western Railway (the prefix to avoid confusion with its mighty neighbour) of whose timber and plaster mock Tudor architecture it is typical. Before the opening of the Settle & Carlisle Clapham was an important junction as the Midland's Scottish traffic passed through. By the turn of the century when this photograph was taken, however, its importance had diminished.
Authors' Collection

Plate 138. Upton-on-Severn, on the same line, shows very little commonality with Ripple. Note the very ornate brickwork and ridge tiles in this turn of the century postcard view.
Authors' Collection

Plate 139. The more solid looking Studley and Astwood Bank station was on the Evesham and Redditch portion of the line opened between 1866 and 1868.
Lens of Sutton

Plate 140. The very neat station at Moseley on the Birmingham & Gloucester line opened in 1867 when the original Moseley station was renamed King's Heath.
R.J. Essery Collection

Plates 141 & 142. Two views of the splendid station at Mansfield which, although having the appearance of a terminus, is in fact a through station. The original terminus closed in 1872 prior to the building of the Mansfield–Worksop line which opened in 1875. These photographs, probably taken at the line's opening, show the imposing station forecourt and facade and the Crystal Palace style trainshed. *P.R. Bunce Collection*

Plates 143 & 144. Mansfield Woodhouse, the first station out of Mansfield on the Worksop line, seen just after the line's opening in 1875 whilst ballasting work was still in progress. There are many details worthy of study such as the wooden platforms, signalbox, slotted post signals and ballast level. *P.R. Bunce Collection*

Plate 145. Lowdham station on the Nottingham–Newark line. Another example of a bay window on the platform, this time on the station building itself, can be seen in this view *circa* 1910. *Lens of Sutton*

Plate 146. The charmingly rural scene at Rearsby between Syston and Melton Mowbray. The covered carriage truck is interesting, particularly its livery. Compare this vehicle with that in Plate 125 showing one at St. Pancras. *Lens of Sutton*

Plate 147. An H Boilered 4–4–0 and train of mixed carriages storm through Wigston Magna station just south of Leicester *circa* 1910. The station boasts substantial brick buildings with the booking hall situated on the overbridge, covered stairways and individualistically decorated canopy valances. *R.C. Betts Collection*

Plate 148. In 1897 the Norfolk and Suffolk Committee was formed to control in lines between Antingham Road Junction (Cromer) and Runton West Junction (West Runton). The Committee consisted of four directors each from the Midland, Great Northern, and Great Eastern railways. The stretch from Mundesley to Roughton Road Junction was opened on 2nd August 1906 when this photograph of Mundesley-on-Sea was taken. The station building is very decorative with a substantial glazed canopy and the platform surfaces are covered with local sand and gravel. *J. Turnbull Collection*

Plate 149. By the late 19th century the Midland's traffic to Ireland had increased to the point where its existing facilities via Barrow on the Furness Railway and Morecambe on the (little) North Western were inadequate. The Midland decided, therefore, to build its own harbour at Heysham complete with quayside passenger station. On 1st September 1904 a boat train service was introduced leaving St. Pancras at 5 p.m. and arriving at Heysham at 10.45 p.m. to connect with the 11 p.m. sailing to Belfast. Other services from Heysham sailed to the Isle of Man, Londonderry and Dublin. This view shows the interior of Heysham station in May 1920 with one of the Lancaster–Morecambe–Heysham electric units alongside the platform. *M.L. Knighton Collection*

DERBY WORKS

The history of Derby Works is as long as that of the Midland Railway itself. Of the three constituent companies, only the Birmingham & Derby Junction did not have its workshops at Derby – initially they were at Hampton-in-Arden, later they moved to Birmingham – and all three possessed engine sheds there. The North Midland's famous sixteen sided engine shed stood opposite Derby station with locomotive and carriage workshops on either side. Next to this complex were the Midland Counties' shed and workshops whilst to the south of the station the Birmingham & Derby Junction Railway built a locomotive shed. All except the latter were destined to be incorporated into the Midland's Derby Works.

At the amalgamation in 1844 Matthew Kirtley – ironically the only one of the three candidates not already based at Derby – was appointed Locomotive & Carriage Superintendent. He found himself in charge of an 8½ acre site containing a total of 2½ acres of Locomotive and Carriage workshops and engine sheds. Kirtley immediately set about improving both the locomotive accommodation and the workshop facilities and in 1874 a second sixteen road roundhouse was built. At this time the Midland bought all its locomotives from outside contractors but Kirtley's aim was to enable the Company to build its own. He managed to convince the Directors of the benefits to be accrued from such capability and by 1851 had expanded the works facilities to the extent that the first Derby built locomotive, single framed 0–6–0 No. 147, was completed in the September. It was followed in December by sister engine No. 146 and in 1852 by two more 0–6–0s and six 2–2–2s. These latter engines were not really new but were hybrid rebuilds of earlier machines based on E.B. Wilson's "Jenny Lind" class with 5ft 6in driving wheels, iron clad boilers and Kirtley designed tenders. Four were joint exercises with Wilson's but two were purely Derby built. Over the succeeding years Derby Works turned out more and more locomotives, though it never attained the capacity to satisfy the Midland's needs in toto and the Company always had to turn to outside contractors. The year 1852 also saw the addition of a further locomotive shed, this year with 24 roads, together with more workshops.

Kirtley's policy of expansion continued through the 1860s and into the 70s, but by the start of the decade he had realised that a major rethink was necessary. To this end he decided that the carriage and wagon shops should be moved to a new site and the existing works should be expanded and reorganised for the Locomotive Department. A new paint shop was built in 1870, but the bulk of the additions and alterations was still outstanding when Kirtley died and it was to his successors, Johnson on the locomotive side and Clayton for carriages and wagons, that the responsibility for carrying out his plans passed. In 1877 both the new carriage & wagon works and the enlarged locomotive works were completed and Derby entered a new era with a greater proportion of its vehicles being built "in house". The two 16 road roundhouses were required for other uses by this time, the old North Midland shed for repairs and the other for stabling spare engines, and plans were drawn up for two 44 road twin turntable sheds. In the event however, only one of them, No. 4 shed, was built and brought into

Plate 150. A variety of engines in assorted states in the old No. 2 erecting shop *circa* 1890. The engines visible are, from nearest the camera, '1357' class Johnson 0–6–0 No. 1462, an unidentified '1070' class 2–4–0 of Kirtley design, Kirtley '700' class 0–6–0 No. 939, Johnson '1142' class 0–6–0 No. 1220, and a further unidentified 2–4–0. No doubt the general tidiness and cleanliness of the workshop areas was specially arranged for the photograph! *Derby Museum*

Plate 151. The boiler shop *circa* 1910. The variety in the appearance of boilers is not so readily appreciable following the addition of all the Midland finery to say the least! *Derby Museum*

Plate 152. A truly marvellous collection of engines outside No. 2 shed of 1847 taken in the closing years of the 1880s. Kirtley types predominate but there is a fair smattering of early Johnson classes amongst them. *Derby Museum*

Plate 153. Taken from the staff footbridge joining the works and the station area, the former Midland Counties Railway engine shed (at that time used as stores) can be seen to the right of this photograph. The road in the centre of the view leads into the former North Midland Railway shed. This view was taken *circa* 1890 looking north. *National Railway Museum*

use in 1890. In addition to all this building the Midland also took over the old Derby Gas Company works and became self sufficient in the Derby area.

By 1900 the 8½ acres which Kirtley had inherited had grown to over 80 acres a quarter of which was covered in buildings, for the locomotive works alone with a 50 acre carriage & wagon works site on the opposite side of the London Main Line. The locomotive works employed nearly 4000 people and were turning out 40 new engines per year, rebuilding and reboilering 120, and carrying out over 800 major repairs. The only other major addition during Midland days was the installation of electric lighting and machinery powered by the works' own generating station in 1910.

Plate 154. A view alongside the erecting shops *circa* 1890. Kirtley classes once again predominate in the row of engines visible. *National Railway Museum*

Plate 155. (facing page) Photographs taken inside the carriage and wagon works are, regrettably, somewhat less in number than those taken of the locomotive works. This view of the lifting shop *circa* 1912 shows several 54 ft. clerestory vehicles, the nearest one being Midland and Glasgow & South Western third class carriage No. 216. This is also a particularly good view of the then recently introduced overhead cranes built by Craven Brothers Limited of Manchester in 1910 (as their cast plates proclaim). *National Railway Museum*

SIGNALLING

Almost every aspect of railways has a direct effect on the safety not only of railway employees but also of the public, and none more so than signalling. No matter how well permanent way, structures and rolling stock are built and maintained or trains are driven, the efficiency of signalling is the ultimate safeguard. From the earliest days of flag carrying policemen (hence the railwayman's term "bobby" for a signalman) to modern power boxes controlling many miles of track, the subject is a complex and fascinating one. Even the history of Midland signalling would require a large volume to do it justice and we hope that one day such a work may appear.

In 1895 the Midland had 12,976 signals which meant an average of 9.7 signals per mile of track. This figure is a reflection on the widespread nature of the system as comparison with the GWR's 5 per mile and the L&YR's amazing 21.7 per mile will illustrate. The appearance of Midland signal apparatus was as distinctive as that of its locomotives, mainly due to the fact that it was produced by the Company itself from an early stage. At the turn of the century only four railway companies were self sufficient in signal equipment, the other three being the GWR, L&YR and LNWR, and therefore no work of this kind could ignore the subject. Rather than attempt the impossible in a small space, however, we have tried merely to illustrate a few notable aspects.

Plate 156. Slotted post signals were introduced on the Midland, we believe, in the early 1870s. This one stood at Shipley (Leeds Junction) and was photographed *circa* 1877. The colour scheme was chocolate or Venetian red up to approximately 4 ft. above ground level and probably lemon chrome above that. The signal lamps were gas lit. *BR*

Plate 157. The hammer shaped "calling on" arm is believed to have first been used on the Midland at Nottingham in 1904, which is the date and location of this photograph. Note the lack of a roundel on the arm.
R.J. Essery Collection

Plate 158. This view of the up distant at Longstone, on the Peak Forest Line, in May 1908 illustrates several aspects of Midland signal practice. The tapered wooden post, fluted finial and wooden arm were standard hallmarks as was the white roundel, or dot, on the arm. This was discontinued in 1906, though the change was obviously not effected overnight, in favour of the more common vertical stripe. The signal arm was painted red, the only difference between the fronts of home and distant signals being the cutout at the end, and the colour scheme of the post was the same as that in plate 157.
M.L. Knighton Collection

Plate 159. The large gantry at Derby station in June 1903. As well as the white roundel referred to in plate 157, this view also shows that the reverse of home signals had black roundels and those of distants a black horizontal stripe. The former was changed to a black vertical stripe in 1906, but distant signals did not follow suit until 1911. Some of the arms have route indications, such as P for passenger lines and G for goods routes, in place of the roundels. The array of point rodding and its routing under the turnout is also of interest. *M.L. Knighton Collection*

Plate 160. More details of point rodding and signal wires can be seen in the foreground of this photograph of St. Pancras Junction *circa* 1905. As can be seen on the two gantries, calling on arms were sited below home and distant signals. Note also that the ends of home arms were curved slightly. The open carriage truck and its load behind a rebuilt Kirtley '690' class 0–4–4 well tank is interesting. *BR*

Plate 161. William Marriot, chief engineer at the M&GN's Melton works, was responsible for much development of the use of concrete and ferroconcrete for railway applications. Between June 1916 and May 1917 he turned his attention to producing signal posts in concrete, which were used not only on the M&GN but also the Midland, Great Central and Great Northern. As well as this one at Derby there were examples at Kegworth and in the Birmingham area. The picture also illustrates well the Acfield pattern steel signal arm, which came into use around 1914, and the wire stays supporting the post. Note also the gantry in the background.
M.L. Knighton Collection

31 DERBY OCT 10 1917

Plate 162. From 1906, when Acfield became signal superintendent, there were several major changes. This photograph shows the main gantry at St. Pancras in 1914 shortly after the modifications previously described. As can be seen, the vertical stripes were applied to calling on arms as well as others. The arms themselves were among the first pressed steel ones used. *A. Brown Collection*

Plate 163. When the signalling failed to achieve its desired effect the results could be spectacular. On 3rd March 1888 a Manchester–Leicester goods train ran into a Derby–York goods train whilst the engine was shunting by Ambergate South Junction signal box. Apart from the obvious mayhem, the picture illustrates well a typical period I box. *Authors Collection*

Plate 164. Midland signal boxes were almost always constructed from timber in standard panels, the size of the box being determined by its location. They were very distinctive structures and there were three basic types, or periods, which although essentially similar were distinguished by their window sizes. From about 1870 there were signal boxes on the Railway, but little is known of them and they are not normally included in the "standard" list. It is believed that they were similar to period I boxes which were built from about 1880 and had windows down to waist level only; very few of them lasted into LMS days. Concurrent with the adoption of block telegraph working around 1890, period II boxes appeared in which the side windows were extended almost to floor level, and this type was built for many years. In 1900 the final type, or period III, box was introduced though period II ones continued to be built for some time. Period III boxes had full length windows on all faces and were built until 1925. This photograph shows a classic example of a period II box at Addingham *circa* 1900 with the station staff. *D.J. White Collection*

Plate 165. A variation on period II design was Rowsley Down Sidings box. The glazing extended all round the cabin to allow the signalman an unrestricted view of the surrounding tracks. Due to the latter's proximity the cabin was one window narrower than usual and there was no outside catwalk. It must have been quite a job leaning out from an open window to clean the others! The small oval plate by the signalman's head denoted the condition of the telegraphic instruments. Hung as shown here with its blue face outward it meant that they were functional; with its long axis vertical and black face showing it indicated a fault. The structure to the right is a rather unusual example of a shunter's platform; a more normal type can be seen on the left of the picture. The head shunter signalled shunting movements with his arms from these platforms.
D. Kingman Collection

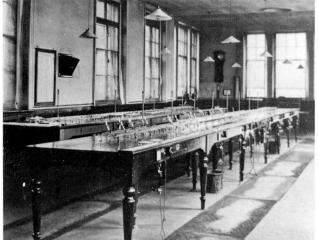

Plate 166. (left) The majority of railway trades received nearly all their training "on the job" without classroom instruction. With the introduction of block working, telegraphs, interlocking etc. this was not feasible for signalmen and a signalling school was established at Derby. This view shows a signal instruction classroom for training in block working.
Authors' Collection

Plate 167. (right) Ambergate Station Junction signalbox with police and military escort during the railway strike of 18th & 19th August 1911. This is another good example of a period II box.
M.L. Knighton Collection

Plate 168. (below) The interior of St. Pancras signalbox which although larger than average shows typical lever frames and block instruments used by the Midland. Note the lever frame at the left hand side of the far end of the cabin. *J. Turnbull Collection*

Plate 169. The unusual turnover pattern lever frame at Rowsley down sidings on 16th August 1917. The levers can just be seen through the windows of the box in plate 165. Levers of this type were sometimes used at siding locations but why and when they were installed is not known. The levers and the pulleys to which they were attached appear to be cast iron and give the impression of being more difficult to use than the conventional ones at the far end. Note the heavy wooden beam at the front of the cabin against which the levers rest. The shelf supporting the block instruments is of a type common in Midland boxes.
M.L. Knighton Collection

WAY AND WORKS

There is an old army recruit saying, "If it moves, salute it; if it doesn't move, paint it". In 1844 the Midland's version could well have been, "If it moves, it's Kirtley's; if it doesn't move, it's Barlow's". William Henry Barlow was the first Chief Engineer of the Midland and though he was theoretically answerable to Robert Stephenson, nominally engineer-in-chief until his death in 1859, in actual fact he was in charge of the Way and Works Department. Virtually all the Company's real property (or "hardware" in modern parlance) except locomotives, rolling stock and signals was under the care and maintenance of the department. Policy was set by the Way and Works Committee and carried out by the Chief Engineer who was in direct control of all but two subsidiary organisations, those run by the Electrical Engineer and the Estates Agent.

Apart from these subsidiaries the department was divided into two sections, new works and maintenance. The latter was sub-divided into three divisions; Northern and Southern, with Derby as the point of separation, and South Wales. The day to day responsibility for examining the railway and directing maintenance effort rested, in 1890, on the shoulders of 43 inspectors who between them had to walk the entire length of the system, identify work required, supervise the men carrying out the resulting tasks, re-inspect the site after-

wards and make sure that everyone in the department had the entire Way and Works rule book read to him twice a year! Obviously these few men could not keep an eye on everything at once, and the day to day inspection of the Permanent way was the responsibility of foremen gangers, each of whom had a length of line, somewhere between ½ and 5 miles generally, which he had to walk over and examine twice every weekday and once on Sunday if passenger trains ran over it.

In addition to his normal duties, each man in the department had to be instantly available 24 hours a day in case of emergency; for this purpose the district inspectors maintained a register of addresses of all the men in their charge. When fog or snow threatened to bring chaos they could be seconded to the Traffic Department as fogsignalmen or snow clearers. Life must often have been difficult for those employed on way and works. To cover the entire activities of the Way and Works Department would require many volumes. In this section, therefore, we will restrict ourselves to illustrating a handful of the lesser publicised and more interesting aspects of this colossal organisation. The emphasis on permanent way is due to the influence of our colleague Mr. Adrian "Track" Tester for whose help we are extremely grateful.

Plate 170. A permanent way gang relaying track near Yate on the one-time broad gauge Bristol and Gloucester line. The view looks towards Wickwar Tunnel and was taken between 1884 and 1888 when it appeared as an engraving in F.S. Williams' *Midland Railway, Its Rise & Progress.* The up line has previously been relaid with 24 ft. rails on inside-keyed chairs whilst the down line is being relaid using 85 lb. 30 ft. rails with outside keys. The remains of the replaced track can be seen; it consisted of 20 ft. rails on inside-keyed chairs with a two spike fixing and seven sleepers per rail length. Note the lookout to the left of the track in the middle distance wearing an armband and behind him the gauge for maintaining the six-foot way between adjacent tracks. The age-old pastime of watching men at work is also evident. *A.P. Tester Collection*

Plate 171. Between the late 1870s and the mid-1890s the Midland undertook a major programme of widening works on many of its routes. This photograph shows such work in progress near Leicester in 1891 during demolition of one of the many bridges which had to be lengthened. The track consists of inside-keyed 24 ft rails and in the middle distance is a good example of a slotted post signal with low finial. The wagons present are interesting; on the left hand side are some predecessors of the D.305 goods wagon with only two end planks and almost certainly equipped with wooden brake blocks, whilst next to them are some early 6 ton low sided wagons, easily recognised by the lack of end stanchions and early design of brake gear. They belong to the engineer's department and have protective tarpaulin covers on the axleboxes; the 6 tonners also have 5 link couplings. On the right of the picture is a crude contractor's wagon. *BR*

Plate 172. The same location as that seen in plate 171 viewed from the opposite direction *circa* 1900. The slotted post signal has gone and a gantry spans the tracks on the far side of the new bridge. On the right stands a rake of 3-plank dropside engineer's department wagons similar to those seen in the previous picture. The track on which they stand has been recently, though not yet properly, ballasted. *BR*

Plate 173. The then recently completed bridge over the River Derwent at Belper seen during the last year of the 19th century. The bridge was reconstructed as part of the rebuilding programme carried through by Mr. McDonald. It is a three span, presumably steel, underbridge consisting of three sets of fabricated main girders supported on stone abutments on the banks, and steel piers, probably filled with concrete, in the river. The piers are braced with lattice girders and the deck rests on cross girders, the ends of which can be seen above the main girders. The parapets, stiffened with ornamented side brackets, are also in lattice style and give a pleasing lightness of appearance to the structure as does the colour scheme of cream and brown. The permanent way consists of 85 lb. 30 ft. outside-keyed track conventionally-ballasted. *M.L. Knighton Collection*

Plate 174. During the widening of the London extension, major civil engineering work was carried out in crossing, amongst other things, the river Lea at Chiltern Green. The style of bridge detail is similar to that shown on page 105. There are many items of interest in this picture including the dress and equipment of the workmen, the windlass and gin winch being used, and the wooden scaffolding and pudlock holes. The track in the foreground is old inside-keyed type and a travelling gantry stands astride the new bridge structure. *BR*

Plate 175. Longstone Tunnel, cut through a limestone ridge called Bladestone Edge, looking towards Monsal Dale on 12th May 1908. Because the cutting immediately prior to the tunnel is through rock, there is very little "batter", or slope, to the sides. The tunnel mouth itself also shows little reinforcement and there are no retaining walls. The permanent way is laid with 100 lb. outside-keyed track and wooden cable trunking runs along the left hand side. *M.L. Knighton Collection*

Plate 176. In the early years of the present century Mr. McDonald had overall responsibility for major improvements at Nottingham and Sheffield. The rebuilt Nottingham Station was formally opened in January 1904 but, as this photograph taken on 10th March of that year shows, work still remained to be completed. The picture shows the canopy being erected on one of the platforms. In the foreground is a crossing laid with 100 lb. rail which appears to be a 1 in 8 formation. *M.L. Knighton Collection*

Plate 177. Some of the Midland's inside-keyed track was surprisingly long-lived as shown by the road in the foreground of this view of Manton, probably taken in 1917, which has 24 ft. rails. The main lines to the right, however, have been relaid with 100 lb outside-keyed rails. Among the many items of Midland station furniture which can be seen is an intriguing LB&SCR timetable board on the corner of the station building facing the camera. *M.L. Knighton Collection*

Plate 178. Another view of "Manton for Uppingham", as the gas lamps inform us, taken at the same time as plate 177. The photograph is useful for details of the lattice footbridge with its unusual cast iron balustrades, and the wide barrow crossing. *M.L. Knighton Collection*

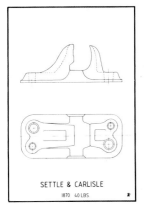
SETTLE & CARLISLE
1870 40 LBS.

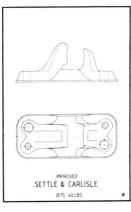
IMPROVED
SETTLE & CARLISLE
1875 40 LBS.

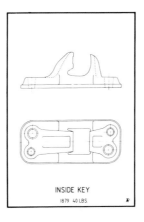
INSIDE KEY
1879 40 LBS.

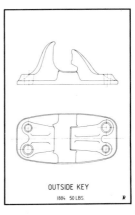
OUTSIDE KEY
1884 50 LBS.

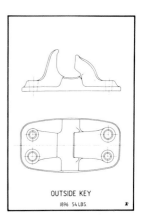
OUTSIDE KEY
1896 54 LBS.

Above. The most commonly recorded types of Midland rail chairs are illustrated in this drawing. The Midland used inside keyed track for many years and the first three illustrations show variations of chairs used on such track. The differences between them were largely concerned with the shape of the foot of the rail in an attempt to overcome a design fault, thought to be cracking of the chairs. They were used mainly with 81 lb. 24 ft. rails, 83 lb. 24 ft. rails and 85 lb. 30 ft. rails.

The ribbed outside key design was introduced in 1884 and used with 85 lb. 30 ft. rails. The drawing is of a revised version, introduced slightly later, which appears to have been more common than the original type.

The 1896 outside-keyed chair was designed for use with the 100 lb. 36 ft. rails introduced at that time. Both this and the previous design became Company standards and remained so for the rest of the Midland's existence. *Drawn by A.P.Tester*

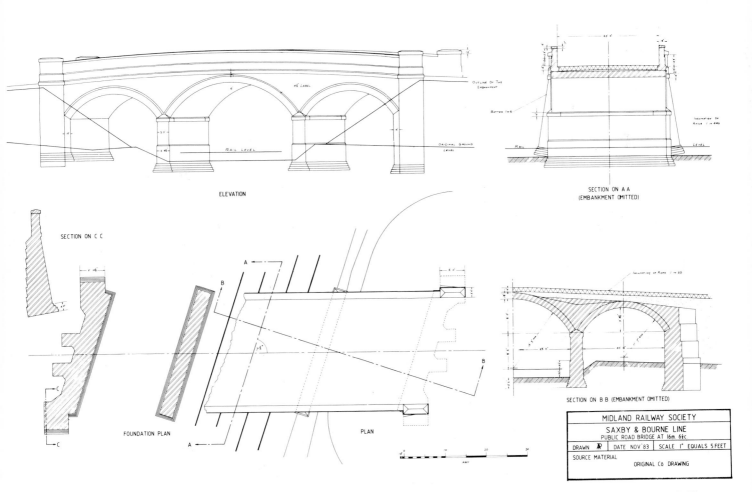

ELEVATION

SECTION ON A A
(EMBANKMENT OMITTED)

SECTION ON C C

FOUNDATION PLAN

PLAN

SECTION ON B B (EMBANKMENT OMITTED)

MIDLAND RAILWAY SOCIETY
SAXBY & BOURNE LINE
PUBLIC ROAD BRIDGE AT 16m. 6¾c.

DRAWN	DATE NOV '83	SCALE 1" EQUALS 5 FEET
SOURCE MATERIAL		
	ORIGINAL C6 DRAWING	

Above. A drawing of one of the bridges erected on the Saxby & Bourne line (opened in May 1894) under the responsibility of the Midland's Chief Engineer Mr.J.A. McDonald. Like many of the Company's overbridges it was of the three arch type with the centre span over the tracks and the side spans on the embankment. Typical of contemporary Midland practice was the use of brick and the 4½ in. label or dripstone, the protruding lip around the top of the arch. *Drawn by A.P. Tester*

CONTINGENCY PLANS

The day-to-day running of the Midland Railway was properly a routine and uneventful business, but from time to time the operating departments had to deal with the unusual, unwanted and unexpected. Fog, snow, landslips, subsidence and flooding were among the natural hazards which had to be overcome, and there was always the possibility that human error could precipitate a derailment or even worse. To deal with such eventualities there existed much specialised equipment, ranging from flags and detonators to breakdown trains, which normally lay idle but by their very nature had to be ready to operate at a moment's notice. Largely unnoticed by the travelling public, due in no small part to the Company's understandable reluctance to widely advertise its existence, such equipment nonetheless formed an important part of the Railway. We only illustrate a small portion of the Midland's large contingency equipment here, but sufficient of it, we hope, to show that it was as distinctive in many ways as the better known stock.

Plate 179. Snowploughs were normally mounted on locomotives or brakevans, but in 1909 it was decided that the Settle and Carlisle line, notorious for snowdrifts, needed something bigger. The result was pair of snowploughs built on Johnson bogie tender frames, rendered obsolete by the introduction of water troughs in 1903. Based at Hellifield they were numbered 1 and 2 and differed only in minor details and the fact that internally No. 1 was fitted for carrying heavy tackle whereas No. 2 carried men. Livery is believed to have been unlined crimson lake with white lettering, possibly shaded black in the case of "LOCO DEPT. HELLIFIELD" and the number. In use they were attached to a pair of 0–6–0s, which were coupled chimney to chimney with the ploughs at each end, and the ensemble then charged the drifts. Apparently they were considered somewhat too light for their job (No. 1 weighed 27 tons 8 cwt tare and No. 2 was 26 tons 1 cwt) and often derailed. They were finally withdrawn by the LMS in the 1930s. *Authors' Collection*

Plate 180. Mobile cranes came in all shapes and sizes, but until at least 1874 all were hand-operated. They ranged from standard goods yard cranes mounted on flat wagons to quite large purpose built types capable of lifting over 10 tons (with the appropriate motive power!).No. 66 was a 5- tonner built by Cowans Sheldon of Carlisle in 1892, though the Midland number plate and instructions for working are dated 1885! Note the folding operating platform, propping girders stowed underneath and the rail clips for fixing the crane whilst operating. *R.J. Essery Collection*

Plate 181. This crane was built by Josiah Booth & Brothers of Rodley near Leeds in 1890 and was allocated to the Southern Division Engineers Dept. at Burton on Trent. At 18 ft. radius its maximum load was 10 tons whereas at 23 ft. 6 in. it was limited to 4 tons. It is attached to match wagon No. 42657. There was only one diagram issued for all match wagons built between 1877 and 1914 – diagram 738 – although the wagons differed even to the extent of wheelbase and overall length. *BR*

Plate 182. The Midland was among the first, if not the first, British railway company to use steam cranes. The first one used was a 5-tonner built by Appleby Brothers of Leicester *circa* 1874, but the most numerous were the Cowans Sheldon 15 ton capacity cranes built between 1893 and 1901. No. 27 was the first one delivered and was initially allocated to Derby where it was photographed when new. They were a standard Cowans Sheldon type except for a shorter than usual jib and lack of self-travelling gear. The maximum jib radius when lifting 15 tons was 22 ft. They were painted crimson lake with white lettering and one of them, No. 28, is recorded as having received black and yellow lining out at one time. *BR*

Plate 183. The Derby breakdown train posed for the camera sometime between 1903 and 1907. The train was kept fully equipped, with steam up on the crane, and when required it would be coupled to the first available suitable locomotive – in this case a '2736' class Johnson 0–6–0. The first vehicle is a Kirtley ballast brake van and the crane and match wagon, Nos. 27 and 114905 respectively, are followed by two vans, probably of Kirtley origin, numbered 9982 and 9984. *BR*

Plate 184. Mining subsidence is mainly caused when props decay and old workings collapse. Colliery companies were under statutory obligation to inform railways before cutting coal from under or close to the latters' tracks. On receipt of such notification the railway would either "buy support", i.e. pay the colliery not to undermine its territory, or set about shoring up its structures. Arches are extremely susceptible to damage by uneven settlement of their supports and unless centring is erected promptly may fail. This view of a bridge at Stockingford near Nuneaton was taken on 26th April 1916 and as can be seen the arches are showing distinct sign of distress. *R.J. Essery Collection*

Plates 185 and 186. To illustrate the effects of subsidence we include these views of Wentworth & Hoyland Common station though no contingency equipment is in view. Taken in June 1911 and November 1913 respectively they show how the platform levels changed following track relaying on two occasions. The area, between Sheffield and Barnsley, must have been a nightmare for the engineers. *M.L. Knighton Collection*

Plates 187 and 188. Two views of a Cowans Sheldon 15 ton crane of the 1893 batch persuading Kirtley '700' class 0–6–0 No. 1045 back onto its rightful place at Breadsall crossing in 1906. The forward extension to the top of the crane's tank is the coal bunker and the propping girders can be seen in place in plate 189. The locomotive appears to be in brown or unlined crimson lake.

A.P. Tester Collection

Plate 189. What happened to a Midland period I signalbox when it had an argument with a Kirtley 0–6–0? The answer can be seen in this picture of Wymondham Junction on 3rd December 1892. The 10 ton hand crane is about to attempt to separate the protagonists whilst the signalman surveys what was once his domain. Note the framing of the unrebuilt Kirtley 2000 gallon tender and the 8 ton dumb-buffered private owner wagon. Between the two is what once was a D.305 plank open wagon. *National Railway Museum*

THE WEST ROAD

The arteries of a railway are its main lines. The beginnings of the Midland system, described earlier, took it to Leeds, Rugby, and Birmingham; by 1923 the arteries stretched from the heart at Derby to Manchester, Carlisle, London, and Bristol as can be seen in the map reproduced at the front of this book. It is with the Birmingham to Bristol section of the latter route that we shall concern ourselves here in order to try to portray the atmosphere of a Midland main line during the 1900 to 1923 period of the Company.

On 13th December 1824 a meeting at the White Lion Inn, Bristol, was held to promote a railway from Bristol via Gloucester, Tewkesbury, and Worcester to Birmingham. The undertaking was known as the Bristol, Northern and Western Railway (BNWR) and was enthusiastically supported; the 1¼ million subscription list was rapidly filled and the future looked bright. By early 1826, however, a combination of engineering difficulties and a financial crisis had shaken the shareholders' confidence and on 19th May the project was abandoned.

In 1828 local interests succeeded in gaining Parliamentary sanction for two horse drawn tramways in the Bristol area – the Avon & Gloucestershire and the Bristol & Gloucestershire, the latter running from Coalpit Heath via Shortwood to the Bristol docks. This line was to play an important part in subsequent developments, as we shall see later, and was opened in 1835.

In 1832 I.K. Brunel was employed to survey a route between Birmingham and Gloucester. The main criterion for the survey was that the line should be as cheap as possible to construct and the route Brunel chose lay well to the east of the present line. Before long, however, financial constraints and administrative difficulties led to a suspension of the scheme and Brunel left. He was succeeded by Captain W.S. Moorsom whose remuneration from the impecunious undertaking was to be linked directly to the results he achieved; thus the chosen route was a combination of directness and avoidance of major towns where land was expensive. One such town was Cheltenham but such an outcry ensued that Moorsom was persuaded to divert the line to include the offended spa. The promise of extra revenue to be derived from Cheltenham must have been considerable as the deviation raised the estimated cost of the line from £750,000 to £950,000, despite the fact that from Cheltenham to Gloucester the Birmingham and Gloucester was to share the route of an old tramway, built in 1809, with the newly promoted Cheltenham and Great Western Union Railway (C&GWU). The Birmingham and Gloucester Railway Bill received Royal Assent on 22nd April 1836 amid the euphoria of the first railway boom. By the end of the year, however, economic conditions had deteriorated and the directors had to steer the Company through many difficult and near ruinous crises which were not helped by the C&GWU's initial tardiness in commencing work on the Cheltenham to Gloucester section. Eventually, however, all the difficulties were overcome and the

Cheltenham to Bromsgrove section was opened on 24th June 1840. By August 1841 the line was open through to Camp Hill; a junction was effected with the London and Birmingham Railway and under the terms of the Birmingham and Gloucester Railway Act its trains were able to run into the London and Birmingham Railway's Curzon Street terminus which was nearing completion. The wording of the Act in fact gave the Birmingham and Gloucester access to any future London and Birmingham terminus "in or near Birmingham": thus the Midland was able to run into the LNWR's New Street station nearly twenty years later.

During the early 1830s railway interest in Bristol was still high and the Bristol merchants looked towards the then newly–promoted Birmingham and Gloucester to give them access to the rich hinterland of the Stephenson lines to the north. To achieve this they planned to extend the Bristol and Gloucestershire tramway to Gloucester and a Bill was presented to Parliament in 1837 but due to strong opposition, orchestrated by a rival group based in Gloucester, it failed. Differences between the two parties were soon ironed out, however, and they combined to present successfully the Bristol & Gloucester Railway Bill to Parliament in 1839. The new scheme also extended the Bristol & Gloucestershire line from Westerleigh but instead of running directly to Gloucester it formed a junction at Standish with the broad gauge Cheltenham & Great Western Union and ran into the county town on mixed gauge tracks. By 1843 the C&GWU had passed into the hands of the Great Western Railway who were also laying siege to the Bristol end of the Bristol and Gloucester. Bowing to the pressure of the GWR the Bristol and Gloucester agreed to make a physical connection at Bristol, to subscribe to the South Devon Railway and to lay their tracks to broad gauge standards; the broad gauge was on the march towards Stephenson country and shudders were felt in many "narrow" gauge boardrooms. On 6th July 1844 the Bristol and Gloucester Railway was formally opened from Bristol Temple Meads amid severe financial gloom and with the spectre of GWR takeover hanging over it.

The Bristol merchants thus had their route to the north, but with one major problem – the notorious "break of gauge" at Gloucester. The gauge question was assuming such proportions that Parliament began seriously to examine it. A committee was sent to Gloucester to see for themselves the difficulties experienced there and thanks to the Birmingham and Gloucester's goods manager, Mr.J.D. Payne, they were not disappointed. Wishing to leave the committee with a lasting impression of the difficulties goods transshipment involved, Payne had two goods trains simultaneously unloaded and then reloaded. The ensuing chaos "beggared the imagination" and the Parliamentarians duly reported to Westminster on the unacceptable situation at Gloucester. Parliamentary opinion was thus strongly in favour of a unified gauge between Bristol and Birmingham and the broad gauge party were quick to try and seize the opportunity of thrusting into the heart of the narrow gauge camp.

Terms for the union of the Bristol and Gloucester and the Birmingham and Gloucester companies had been reached in 1844 and a Bill to this effect was presented to Parliament in January 1845 but was held up due to failure to comply with Standing Orders. Notwithstanding this, the two companies came under joint management as from 14th January and the broad gauge, in the shape of the GWR, made its move. Offering the Birmingham and Gloucester's shareholders 60 of GWR stock for each 100 of Birmingham and Gloucester stock the GWR waited for the plum to drop as, with the stock prices then in force, they were effectively offering £123 for every £109. The Birmingham and Gloucester shareholders, however, wanted 65 of GWR stock and the GWR deferred a decision for three days. During this period one of the greatest coups of railway history was made. The story goes that purely by chance John Ellis, deputy chairman of the Midland, found himself in a compartment with two Birmingham and Gloucester directors discussing the situation. Whether or not this meeting was purely a chance one seems somewhat unlikely at this point in time, but no other evidence has yet appeared to the contrary! On his own responsibility Ellis pledged that if the GWR talks failed the Midland would lease the Bristol and Birmingham line at an annual rental of 6% and settle all outstanding liabilities. The GWR refused to increase its offer and to its astonishment

found that the plum that was so ripe for picking fell three days later to the opposition. On 30th January 1846 the Midland leased the Bristol and Birmingham line in perpetuity as from 30th July, and on 3rd August 1846 the Midland Amalgamation Act transferred ownership to Derby. Thus the redoubtable Ellis, later to steer the company through the difficulties following the Hudson debacle, stemmed the broad gauge tide at Gloucester.

Break of gauge, of course, still plagued the system and on 14th August 1848 the Midland gained the Royal Assent for an Act empowering it to build an independent line from Gloucester to Stonehouse, thus avoiding the GWR's line from Standish Junction, and to lay mixed gauge tracks from there to Bristol. The standard gauge rails came into use on 29th May 1854 and the broad gauge metals were eventually removed in 1872. By 1857 all the Midland's broad gauge equipment had been converted, broken up or sold off and Birmingham to Bristol traffic was exclusively standard gauge. One additional benefit accrued to the Midland from the machinations of 1845. The LNWR were so anxious to stem the broad gauge spread into the Midlands that they offered to share with the Midland any losses incurred in the latter's leasing and subsequent purchase of the Bristol line; this was later modified to a nominal £100 a year rent for the use of New Street station in Birmingham.

Plate 190. New Street station was built by the LNWR and opened officially on 1st June 1854. From its opening the Midland were tenants and the Midland side of the station is seen here on 29th August 1912. The locomotive is Fowler '483' class 4-4-0 No. 498 which had only just entered service when the photograph was taken as a renewal of one of Johnson's H boilered 4-4-0s. *W.L. Good*

Plate 191. Moseley was one of the original stations on the Birmingham & Gloucester Railway opened in 1840. In 1867 it was renamed King's Heath and a new Moseley station was built further to the south; it is the latter which is shown in this view looking north towards Birmingham about 1910. The train consists of one of the Birmingham district suburban sets built in 1908–9. Both Moseley and King's Heath closed in 1941. *Authors' Collection*

Plate 192. The original B&GR line from Birmingham via Camp Hill and King's Heath was not destined to remain the Midland's only route south out of the City. In 1876 the Birmingham West Suburban Railway was opened from Five Ways via Selly Oak to a junction with the Birmingham & Gloucester line at King's Norton and in 1885 it was extended to Birmingham Central and New Street. One peculiarity which resulted was that southbound Manchester–Bournemouth expresses (introduced in 1910), routed via Camp Hill, ran the same way through the same New Street platform as the northbound Bournemouth–Manchester trains which used the Selly Oak line! This picture was taken at Church Road on the Birmingham West Suburban line in 1908 and shows a Bristol bound express running through – the first stop after New Street for these trains would have been King's Norton, Northfield or Barnt Green. The train originated at York and at this stage in its journey was being hauled by '1853' class Johnson 4–2–2 No. 633 built in 1892. *C.B. Harley*

Plate 193. King's Norton was an important junction between the two routes south west out of Birmingham and the timetable shows a large number of express and suburban trains stopping there. In this view, taken in 1924, '483' class 4–4–0 No. 513 approaches the up platform with a Bristol–Birmingham express. The station buildings are to the same pattern as those seen in the view of Moseley at plate 191 and were erected about 1876. The station was rebuilt in 1926 when the LMS quadrupled the line. *R.S. Carpenter Collection*

Plate 194. A West of England express pauses at King's Norton on 21st August 1912. The locomotive is of interest as it is one of the few Johnson "Slim boilered" 4–4–0s to avoid rebuilding or renewal as a '483' class and furthermore, received an extended smokebox in 1909, possibly making it unique. *W.L. Good*

Plate 195. Two 2–4–0s on the quadruple-tracked section of the line near Northfield on 1st October 1921. To the north of Northfield the B&G and Birmingham West Suburban lines met at King's Norton whilst immediately to the south the line to GWR territory turned away to the west at Northfield Junction. Beyond this the line "down the ditch" left the B&G at Barnt Green to run via Alvechurch, Redditch and Evesham. Thus the section of line through Northfield was often quite congested and scenes such as this were common. No. 19 was built as one of Kirtley's '156' class in 1868 and is seen here on a local working being overtaken by an express headed by No. 279, originally Johnson '1492' class No. 1499 of 1881. Both locomotives have been rebuilt with Deeley smokeboxes but retain the Johnson style continuous handrails. Note that the 2 signal posts visible in the photograph are of Marriot's concrete type then only recently introduced in the Birmingham Area (see plate 161). *W.L. Good*

Plate 196. A common sight at Blackwell was that of a goods guard pinning down the wagon brakes before his train made its cautious way down the Lickey incline. In this view, however, the crew of 'H' boilered 0–6–0 No. 3604 are ensuring that the tender brakes of their dead locomotive train are on before what must have been a fairly hazardous descent. No. 5604 is in fact, in charge of five Fowler class 4 goods engines built by Armstrong Whitworth & Co.in April 1922 and being delivered to the S&DJR where they became nos. 57–61. *Authors' Collection*

Plate 197. One of Mr. Kirtley's '890' class 2–4–0s with its post-1907 number 120 leaving Blackwell in July 1921 in charge of a Bristol–Bradford train. The leading vehicle is one of the D.550 6-wheeled clerestory full brakes built for the service in 1897 along with the other 8-wheeled carriages in the train. *W.L. Good*

Plate 198. Blackwell stands at the top of the notorious Lickey Incline, the scene of much banking activity in steam days. This photograph, taken in 1913, shows new '483' class 4–4–0 No. 517 hauling a Bristol express past two banking engines waiting to return to Bromsgrove after assisting a train up the incline. The bankers are 0–6–0Ts built by the Vulcan Foundry. No. 1947 was delivered in 1902 as a condensing engine and survived until 1959, receiving a Belpaire G 5½ boiler and 4 ft 7 in wheels in 1925. Other points of interest include the ground signal and point rodding in the foreground and the young enthusiasts engrossed in watching the 4–4–0. *Authors' Collection*

Plate 199. Bromsgrove in the early years of the present century showing the sharp transition to the 1 in 37 of the Lickey Incline at the far end of the platforms. Note the track layout enabling Bristol bound trains to run through the station on the middle road. The buildings behind the Bristol platform are the wagon building shop & iron store and the spring & machine shop belonging to the Bromsgrove wagon works. *Authors' Collection*

Plate 200. One of the most famous Midland locomotives was the 0–10–0 Lickey Banker, the largest engine the Company possessed. Also known as "Big Bertha" after the World War I rail mounted gun she was built to one of four designs prepared in 1912 to meet the requirement for "super power" to assist trains up the two miles of 1 in 37 from Bromsgrove to Blackwell. She was ordered in 1914 but the war interrupted her development and delivery did not take place until the end of 1919 when she replaced two of the 0–6–0Ts seen in Plate 198. This view illustrates well the large, steeply inclined 16¾ in x 28 in outside cylinders – two more of the same size were positioned between the frames. Because of the length of the G105 boiler, drivers had difficulty buffering up to trains so a large electric headlight was fitted in 1921 which dates this picture sometime during 1920. The photograph is also useful as a good illustration of footplatemen's garb of the period.
R.S. Carpenter Collection

Plate 201. A study of this photograph, in particular the gentlemen on the footplate and various marks on the front of the engine, would suggest that it was taken on the same day as Plate 200. It purports to show No. 2290 performing its duties banking a train up the incline but the poses of the crew and the gap between locomotive and brakevan buffers seem to indicate that it is a posed tableau for the camera. As a point of interest, Bertha's chimney was second-hand having been taken from the ill-starred Paget locomotive. *Authors' Collection*

Plate 202. Gloucester was the meeting point of the two Companies which originally formed the Birmingham–Bristol line as previously described. It was always an important station and the majority of trains stopped there. This 1913 photograph shows a West of England express hauled by Johnson 7 ft 4 in 'single' No. 614 built in 1899 standing in the platform advertised by the footbridge as being for "The West of England, Bristol, Bath and Bournemouth". The fireman is leaning out of the cab watching for the "right away" from the guard. *R.S. Carpenter Collection*

Plate 203. The 10.55 am ex Derby arriving at Gloucester behind eight year old 4–4–0 No. 771. To the right stand 7 ft 4 in Single No. 604 and 'H' boilered 4–4–0 No. 538 waiting to take trains forward to Bristol. Beyond No. 604 is a cattle wagon showing the large amounts of limewash used to disinfect such vehicles at this time. A close scrutiny of the signals visible above the cattle wagon suggests that one of the arms has been repainted with a black stripe on its rear whilst the one showing clear retains the Midland "black spot"! *C.B. Harley*

NORTH WEST FROM AMBERGATE

The Peak District of Derbyshire is probably one of the most beautiful parts of the British Isles. Leaving the industrial Midlands the landscape begins to blend into green valleys and tree- clad slopes; small villages steeped in history abound before another change of scenery in the north of the district reveals high areas of remote moorland and deep gorges cut through limestone crags. Since prehistory the area has been crossed by important trade routes, particularly those bringing salt form the Cheshire plain to Eastern England. In the nineteenth century there were many schemes to project railways through the Peak District but few succeeded.

The most important proposal was for a line from Stockport on the Manchester & Birmingham Railway, via Buxton and Matlock, to the Midland Railway at Ambergate. Both these railways supported the newcomer but as soon as the M&BR became part of the London & North Western, support from that direction was withdrawn. In other words the mandarins at Euston Square pursued a policy of keeping the Midland out of Manchester at all costs. The only section of the line – with the long title of the Manchester, Buxton, Matlock and Midlands Junction Railway – ever built was from Ambergate to Rowsley opened in 1849. Known as "the little railway with the long name" it was leased jointly by the Midland and LNWR for a period of 19 years from 1852. The Midland began to look at various schemes to extend from Rowsley towards Manchester. The issue resolved finally around Buxton. Both the LNWR and Manchester Sheffield & Lincolnshire Railway (later the Great Central) wished to project lines from their existing branches to that town, whilst the Midland regarded it as a stepping stone to Manchester. The Act of Parliament for the Midland's Rowsley to Buxton line was obtained in 1860 and Buxton reached in 1863 at about the time the LNWR entered the town from Stockport via Whaley Bridge.

The problem was how to get from Buxton to Manchester. Considered routes were either blocked by the LNWR and MS&L or totally impracticable from an operating point of view. By one of those chances which history occasionally allows, a party of Midland officers surveying the area met a party from the MS&L doing the same thing. In a rare moment of railway cooperation, partially caused by the poor financial position of the MS&L, they decided to join forces and the Midland, in exchange for allowing the MS&L onto various parts of its system, gained access over the latter's tracks from New Mills into Manchester. The way was open! The new route left the Buxton line just north of Millers Dale and passed by way of Great Rocks Dale, Peak Forest, Dove Holes, Chapel-en-le-Frith and New Mills where it made a junction with the MS&L, having taken over abandoned works of the latter from Bugsworth and Gowhole towards New Mills.

Opposition to the line came from Ruskin, whose pet hate was the steam railway, describing it thus, "In those clefts every charm depends on the alternate jut and recess of rock and field, on the successive discovery of blanched height and wooded hollow, and above all on the floriated banks and foam crisped wavelets on the sweetly willful stream.Into the very heart and depth of this, and mercilessly bending with the bends of it, your railway drags its close-clinging damnation".

Furthermore, he said, the only achievement would be that, "Every fool in Buxton can be in Bakewell in half an hour and every fool in Bakewell at Buxton; which you think a lucrative process of exchange – you Fools Everywhere". The Duke of Rutland objected to the line passing within sight of Haddon Hall, and a costly and partially unnecessary tunnel was built beneath the grounds so that his Grace would not be offended. The tunnel was mostly "cut and cover", construction gave enormous problems, and heavy rainfall in 1861 led to its partial collapse with five men being killed. The line was opened from Rowsley to Hassop in 1862 and to Buxton in 1863. In 1867 the link to New Mills was completed and Midland trains began to run over the MS&L into Manchester.

It was an extremely costly line to build and involved many tunnels, viaducts, bridges and earthworks. Throughout its existence the severe gradients caused headaches for the operating staff and sweat for the footplate crews who had to get the trains over the Peak. It was one of the most impressive pieces of railway engineering in the country and the scenery viewed from a carriage window was breathtaking. Some of the views to which the traveller was treated had only been seen by a handful of people before, and never in such comfort, and the line was long a Mecca for railway enthusiasts.

There was, however, still a problem to be faced. The LNWR had an interest in the Ambergate to Rowsley portion of the line and the lease was due to expire in 1871. What would happen if Euston gained control? The Midland would be left with a line from Rowsley to New Mills unconnected with the parent system; thus a cut-off line was proposed from Wirksworth to Rowsley, the Duffield–Wirksworth branch having already been authorised in 1863. At the height of the Midland's agonies, however, the LNWR withdrew from the MBM&MJR and left the Midland in sole charge; the little railway with the long name became part of the Midland Railway in 1871. All was now clear, immediate improvements took place and the Midland was left to operate its hard- won line in peace, Wirksworth remaining a branch terminus (see plates 232 & 233). Eventually the Midland constructed a cut-off line from New Mills via Hazel Grove and Cheadle heath to Manchester Central and thus secured its own route throughout.

Plate 204. Matlock Bath station looking north up the Derwent Valley about the turn of the century. An unidentified Johnson 4–4–0 passes through with an up express whilst a slow train pulls out of the platform towards Matlock. The wooden goods shed on a brick plinth was of a type seen elsewhere on the Midland. It was very soundly-constructed and survived until it was demolished in May 1984 to make way for yet more cars to be parked. The double slip in the foreground was a common feature of Midland station track layouts away from the running lines. Turnouts on running lines were nearly always trailing as seen here; the Midland had a strong dislike for facing points. *Authors' Collection*

Plate 205. A closer view of Matlock Bath station which shows that although the signal box and lattice footbridge were common Midland designs the station buildings were unique. Their Swiss chalet style was in keeping with the tourist name of "The Switzerland of England". The buildings on the down platform still exist at the time of writing, the main one being in use until recently as a cafe, and are now owned by Derbyshire Dales District Council. *Authors' Collection*

Plate 207. (facing page, above) The stately proportions of Monsal Dale viaduct can be appreciated in this view taken in June 1915 from the Wye Valley. The arch on the right hand side was rebuilt about 1906 following a landslip caused, we understand, by a small earth tremor. *M.L. Knighton Collection*

Plate 208. (facing page, below) Monsal Dale station was the subject of the following epithet shortly after its opening: "There is not in the whole range of Peak scenery such a lovely landscape in so small a space as can be viewed from the platform of this singular and romantically situated station". Initially it was only intended to have a goods station on the site to serve nearby Cressbrook Mill, but an official change of heart led to the passenger station being built and opened on Saturday 1st September 1866. The name appears to have been the subject of some doubt as the names Cressbrook Sidings and Cressbrook both appear in official records before it became Monsal Dale. As can be seen, the down platform was masonry whilst that on the up lines of wood built on piles driven into the hillside. The wooden station buildings were second-hand, the Extra Works Book recording an expenditure of £97/10/0 for taking down the station buildings at Evesham and re-erecting same at Monsal Dale. *BR*

Plate 206. Rowsley station was convenient for the Duke of Devonshire's estate at Chatsworth. In the early years of this century King Edward VII was a guest of the 8th Duke at the famous Chatsworth house parties after spending Christmas at Sandringham. The station was suitably decorated for such Royal occasions. Presumably the shovel against the wall was for last minute emergencies. *BR*

Plates 209 and 210. In 1903 an Act of Parliament was passed authorising the Midland to extend and enlarge Millers Dale station. The goods yard was increased in capacity and loops were installed which required a second set of double tracks to be laid through the station. This layout necessitated the construction of a second viaduct over the River Wye, the steel work for which was made by the Butterley Company of Ripley who also made the St. Pancras train shed roof. The new viaduct opened for traffic on 20th August 1905 and the original one taken out of use for strengthening. This was done by Messrs. Handyside & Co. of Derby at a cost of £6,402/2/0d and the viaduct reopened on 1st April 1906. Plate 209 shows the original viaduct in splendid isolation prior to 1903. The stone for the piers of the new viaduct came from Darley Dale. The two viaducts stand together in plate 210 after all work has been completed in May 1906. *Both M.L. Knighton Collection*

'95 MILLERS DALE MAY 1906.

Plate 211. Although double-headed freight trains were not as endemic as some would have us believe, they were perhaps more common on the Midland than on the vast majority of other railways! This view shows Johnson '1502' class 2–4–0 piloting an unidentified Johnson '1873' class 0–6–0 on a mineral train near Chinley around 1910. Note that the majority of the wagons visible in the train are privately-owned. *Real Photographs*

Plate 212. In June 1915 the Midland Railway official photographer took a series of pictures along the line, this view being described as Monsal Dale. The photograph was taken from the hillside above Cressbrook tunnel looking towards the 515 yard long Litton tunnel. The location is actually known as Water-cum-Joli. *M.L. Knighton Collection*

THE CROMFORD CANAL

During the latter part of the 18th century, the growth of Britain's canal system foreshadowed the great mania years of railway speculation that were to follow over 50 years later. One of the schemes proposed was for a navigation running from the Erewash canal at Langley Mill near Nottingham to Cromford, where Arkwright's mill stood in the Derwent Valley. The inaugural meeting of the Cromford Canal Company was held in the Old Bath Hotel at Matlock Bath (now the site of a car park) on 24th August 1789, and the 14⅝ mile long canal was eventually opened in 1794. The engineers were the famous duo of William Jessop and Benjamin Outram who were partners in the newly-formed Butterley Company.

Across the hills lay the Peak Forest canal and the route to Manchester, and like their railway successors the canal engineers bent their talents to finding a route through the Peak. Supposedly at Outram's suggestion, the idea of a canal involving many flights of locks was abandoned in favour of a tramroad and this eventually took shape as the Cromford & High Peak Railway which joined the route of the Peak Forest Canal at Whaley Bridge. Thus the Cromford Canal and the C&HPR formed links in the through route from Leicester and Nottingham to Manchester which carried mainly coal, coke, lime and iron.

The 1830s and 40s were the busiest years for the canal but the writing was on the wall and as early as 1845 negotiations were under way to sell the undertaking to the Erewash Valley and Manchester Railway. At a special general meeting held on 4th June 1845 the Committee was authorised either to sell to, or amalgamate with, this or any other canal or railway company. In October of that year they entered into negotiations with the Manchester Buxton Matlock & Midlands Junction Railway (our old friend the little railway with the long name) and Royal assent to incorporate it into the railway company was received on 26th July 1846. Unfortunately, the slump following the collapse of the 1845 railway mania intervened and the sale was not actually completed until 1852, by which time the impecunious state of the MBM&MJR had resulted in its being leased jointly to the MR and LNWR. As had been foreseen by the canal proprietors, the opening of the line from Ambergate to Rowsley in 1849 had robbed their line of much of its revenue and it was being used for little more than local traffic. As previously told, the MBM&MJR, and with it the canal, became vested in the Midland Railway in 1871 and so the waterway comes within the scope of this book.

The canal was finally abandoned in 1944 and much of it dried up. Recently, however, the Cromford Canal Society Ltd. has taken over a portion of Ambergate–Cromford section and done much restoration work which has enabled narrow boats once more to navigate part of this historic waterway.

Plate 213. In 1889 a subsidence in Butterley Tunnel resulted in its closure for four years. In the early 1900s a more serious collapse led eventually to its permanent closure in 1909. The tunnel was blocked off and thus the canal was bisected. This photograph was taken on 22nd June 1909 when the canal was drained and work was in progress inside the tunnel. *M.L. Knighton Collection*

Plate 214. A section of the canal near Whatstandwell on 27th February 1920 during repair work following a breach of the bank. In the background is part of the Peak Forest line. Thanks to the efforts of the Cromford Canal Society Ltd this scene still exists though the canal itself looks somewhat different. *M.L. Knighton Collection*

Plate 215. Taken at the same time as plate 213, this view shows work in progress to deepen the sides of the canal whilst the pound is drained. As can be seen from the far bank the sides have silted up considerably. Note the survey pole in the left foreground. *M.L. Knighton Collection*

THE DORE AND CHINLEY LINE

Once the Midland had fought and won its battle for Manchester it began to consider other trans-Pennine traffic, in particular that from Sheffield. The only direct route between the two cities was via Woodhead by the Manchester Sheffield & Lincolnshire Railway (later the Great Central). The Midland's only offering was a roundabout way through Chesterfield, Derby, Ambergate & Chinley and it was anxious to compete on a more even footing. In 1872 a line was proposed from Dore, just south of Sheffield on the route to Chesterfield, to Hassop on the Peak Forest line but the plan was short lived.

Twelve years later the Midland decided to try again and put forward a proposal for another line from Dore, this time passing under Totley Moor into the Hope Valley, thence into the Vale of Edale and through Toot Hill to Chinley where it would join the Peak Forest line. The scheme was successful and powers for construction were granted in 1888. The line was both difficult and costly to build which is not surprising when it is considered that over a quarter of its 21 miles are in tunnels, including the second longest main-line tunnel in the British Isles at Totley – 3 miles 950 yards – and the 2 miles 182 yards of Cowburn, making it Britain's ninth longest. Totley was a very wet tunnel to bore and at one stage over 5 million gallons a day were being pumped out of the workings but eventually the headings met on 23rd October 1892 and by September 1893 work was complete. The construction of this tunnel is described in Brian Edwards' book "Totley and

the Tunnel"§. Cowburn was not as bad although the first shaft sunk filled with water and work had to be carried out in diving bells!

Six years after construction started the line was opened for goods traffic on 6th November 1893. The following April it officially became part of the Midland Railway, ownership until then having been vested in the Dore & Chinley company, and passenger services commenced on 1st June. Chinley station was altered for the line's opening, but with the quadrupling of the tracks to New Mills in 1902 it was decided that it was once more inadequate and a completely new station was built some 400 yards to the west. At the same time Dore & Totley station was being widened and improved – a long overdue activity as the extra traffic due to the Dore & Chinley line had been straining resources since its opening.

The Dore and Chinley Line was known as the "Dore & Chinley Branch" to the Midland Railway engineer, even though it was a well used through route, but it has outlived its prestigious Peak Forest neighbour which was closed to through traffic in 1967. Despite the intermediate stations being reduced to unstaffed halts with small shelters instead of station buildings, trains still run through Totley and Cowburn tunnels and the beautiful scenery can be admired from a carriage window. Indeed, in 1988 the line is being used for a new hourly cross-country service from the North-West to East Anglia.

§ Distributed by Platform 5 Publishing.

Plate 216. Dore & Totley station sometime after 1903 when the lattice girder footbridge was built. The Hope Valley trains used the platform nearest the camera. Note the letter box set into the wall by the gates. *J. Turnbull Collection*

Plate 217. Grindleford station and the western portal of Totley Tunnel *circa* 1900. The station building at the end of the overbridge is still under construction in this view. In Midland days it contained the ticket office and station master's accommodation but is now used as a cafe. *J. Turnbull Collection*

Plate 218. A splendid photograph of Grindleford station taken slightly later than plate 217 from the road along the edge of Padley Wood. The platform shelters were of wooden construction as can be seen on the right of the picture. *J. Turnbull Collection*

Plate 219. Hathersage station looking east in the early 1900s. Note the timber platforms and a host of typical Midland features such as the water tower, gas lamps, station seats etc. *Authors' Collection*

Plate 220. Hope station around the turn of the century. Although the station buildings on the line were all constructed of wood to a similar design, those at Hope were larger than normal reflecting the station's importance. There were extensive goods facilities and some wagons can be seen in the distance. The lattice footbridge, to a standard Midland design, is still standing albeit in a somewhat neglected state. Hope was to have been the junction for a light railway to Castleton for which a light railway order was obtained in 1904, but the only result was a suffix to the station nameboards reading "for Castleton and Bradwell". *BR*

MIDLAND INFLUENCE IN THE MENDIPS

The Midland Railway was joint lessee with the London & South Western of the Somerset & Dorset Joint Railway. The beginnings of the system were the Somerset Central and the Dorset Central Railways opened in 1854 abd 1860 respectively. The former started life as a broad gauge line from Glastonbury to Highbridge where it joined the Bristol & Exeter Railway, who actually operated it, and later extended to Burnham in 1858 and Wells in 1859. The Dorset Central was operated by the LSWR from a junction near Wimborne to Blandford. In 1862 the Somerset Central opened a mixed gauge line from Glastonbury to Cole where it met the newly-built Dorset Central line to Templecombe connecting with the Salisbury and Yeovil Railway. North of Templecombe the Somerset company operated all services with its own standard gauge stock. On 1st September 1862 the two concerns amalgamated to form the Somerset & Dorset Railway although the Dorset Central continued to be operated by the LSWR until August 1863 when the link form Blandford to Templecombe was opened. With running powers from Wimborne to Hamworthy the S&D achieved its Channel to Channel (Bristol & English) route and then extended its southern terminus as the LSWR tracks reached Poole in 1872 and Bournemouth two years later.

The Midland Railway reached Bath in 1869 where the Somerset & Dorset joined it in 1874. By this time, however, the S&D was financially exhausted and operating conditions were a shambles. The Company's reputation was poor to say the least and it became obvious that one or more of the bigger and more secure companies would have to take over. Initially negotiations were opened with the Great Western, but eventually these were closed in favour of jointly leasing the line to the Midland and LSW Railways, which was undertaken for a period of 999 years as from 1st November 1875. The arrangement could not take effect, however, until the Somerset & Dorset Leasing Act of 13th July 1876 and conditions on the line continued to give cause for concern. Ironically, it was a mere 25 days after the Act that these conditions led to the horrific accident at Radstock when 13 people lost their lives and 34 were injured, and public outcry was directed at the new regime.

The two lessees immediately instigated and urgent review of the whole system and, amongst the results, was the allocation of permanent way matters to the LSWR and responsibility for locomotives and rolling stock to Derby. Highbridge Works had been opened in 1862 and from early days had been actively concerned in carriage and wagon construction. Apart from three tank engines built for working the Radstock Colliery branches, however, Highbridge never built any locomotives and after the leasing this situation continued. Locomotives were all built either at Derby or by outside contractors and had the hallmarks of Midland design, though many on them, despite their appearances, were designed specifically for the S&D.

From the leasing, S&DJR locomotives were painted in standard Midland green livery until 1886 when the well-known Highbridge blue was introduced. Four of the Johnson 0-4-4 tanks, Nos. 52–55, were delivered in 1885 in Derby red but were soon repainted. The colour difference does not, of course, show up well in black and white photographs and S&D trains can easily

Plate 221. In 1914 emerged the largest locomotives yet built at Derby although they were, of course, not to be used on the Midland Railway itself. Six of the Clayton-designed 2–8–0s were built there for the Somerset and Dorset Joint Railway numbered 80 to 85. In 1925 a further batch of five locomotives were built by R. Stephenson & Co. Ltd. and numbered 86 to 90. These differed somewhat from the earlier engines in that they had a larger boiler giving them a somewhat ponderous appearance as seen in this view of No. 90 in works grey livery.

be mistaken for their Midland brethren.

That Derby took seriously its responsibilities is witnessed by the fact that the biggest locomotives constructed there in Midland days were (with the exception of the 0–10–0 Lickey Banker) not for the parent system but the jointly-operated outpost in the Mendips.

Plate 222. A Somerset & Dorset train in the LSWR station at Poole *circa* 1900. The locomotive is a Johnson designed 4–4–0 built at Derby between 1891 and 1897 and generally known as the 'A' class. The leading vehicle behind the tender is a Midland clerestory carriage. *Authors' Collection*

Plate 223. Wincanton station with the staff posed on the far platform. The passengers and milk churns suggest that they will soon be busy with a train arriving at the near one. Although the station building is stone there is remarkably little ironwork, the awning supports and footbridge being timber. Wincanton was built by the Dorset Central and was the intermediate station between Templecombe and Cole. *Authors' Collection*

Plate 224. It comes as no great surprise that Somerset & Dorset Joint Railway trains had much in common with those of the Midland. After the London & South Western and Midland Railways jointly took over the "Ishmael of Railways" in 1876, the Midland became responsible for locomotives and passenger stock. A Johnson 0–4–4T is seen here with a stopping train at Spetisbury *circa* 1900. Note the old disc and crossbar signal on the left of this delightful and typically S&DJR scene. *Dr. T.F. Budden*

Plate 225. A very clean and tidy Spetisbury station some years after the view in plate 224. Of interest are the Midland style of platform seat and the combination of Midland, Somerset & Dorset, and London & South Western notice boards on the wall. *Authors' Collection*

Plate 226. The 6-wheeled passenger brake van was a type widely used on the S&DJR and several different designs were built between 1886 and 1903. No. 4 was a 30 ft. arc-roofed variant and is seen here in photographic grey posed for the official photographer, presumably just after being built in, it is believed, 1887. It bears more than a passing resemblance to Clayton 6-wheeled stock built for the Midland. *Authors' Collection*

Plate 227. (facing page, above) One of the class 'A' 4–4–0s seen after rebuilding in August 1904 with an 'H' boiler. The alterations are similar to those made to Johnson's Midland 4–4–0s around the same time. The vehicle behind the tender is a milk van built to virtually the same design for both the Midland and the S&DJR. It is followed by LSWR semi–elliptical roofed stock. *F.W. Shuttleworth Collection*

Plate 228. (facing page, below) The S&DJR 0–4–4 tanks were as commonly used as their Midland counterparts. No. 54 was built in 1885 by the Vulcan Foundry and was reboiled in 1907. It is seen here with Deeley-style chimney and smokebox door shortly before withdrawal in 1920. The rear locomotive was one of a batch of nine built by the Avonside Engine Company in 1877 and given different boilers between 1906 and 1910. Note the Whitaker tablet exchange apparatus fitted to the bunker sides. *Lens of Sutton*

BRANCH LINES

Although the Midland served plenty of out of the way communities it normally managed to do so by way of one of its main or secondary lines and never did possess many branch lines. Quite a number of its routes came into the "secondary" category such as Barnt Green to Ashchurch via Evesham and Redditch, and the Dore & Chinley line. It has been said that the Nottingham–Lincoln route is just a long branch, but we do not wish to enter an argument on these lines (!) Suffice it to say that a book on Midland branches would probably not run to as many volumes as one with a Great Western theme.

Some lines were reduced to branch status on completion of another route; the Bedford–Hitchin line, for example, when the London extension to St. Pancras opened. The Midland was also quick to spot an opportunity for extending its domain when small companies either ran out of money or faced opposition with which they could not compete, and several lines were acquired by stepping into the breach at the opportune moment, e.g., the Dursley branch. Other offshoots were originally intended for greater things such as the cut off line from Bradford which should have carried the Midland's Scotch traffic, but failed through lack of money and never got any further than Dewsbury. Even the Wirksworth branch featured in a scheme for reaching Manchester by way of Rowsley before the Manchester, Buxton, Matlock & Midlands junction Railway route was secured.

Despite the relative lack of branch lines, those of the Midland Railway had plenty of character. Some of that character, we hope, will be evident in the following pages.

Plate 229. A modellers dream! Heath Park Halt, also on the Hemel Hempstead branch, with its tiny wooden platform on the embankment and one-coach branch train. The locomotive is a M&GN 4–4–0 tank and is in charge of a converted Pullman auto-coach. *Authors' Collection*

Plate 230. Redbourn station on the Harpenden to Hemel Hempstead branch, often referred to as the "Nickey" line. The station building and goods shed were timber-built. *Lens of Sutton*

The Station, Idridgehay.

Plate 231. Idridgehay on the Duffield to Wirksworth branch is beautifully illustrated by this turn of century view. The line was built through the picturesque Ecclesbourne Valley and was opened in October 1867. It was originally intended to connect with the Cromford & High Peak Railway just beyond Wirksworth, but it is doubtful if the connection was ever made. *Authors' Collection*

Plate 232. A fine period piece view of Wirksworth in the 1890s. Comparison with Plate 231 will show that the station buildings were virtually identical; in fact all the station buildings on the branch were built to the same design. As can be seen, the yards were quite extensive due to the heavy transshipment of stone from local quarries – traffic which still exists but chokes the local roads and creates havoc in the town instead of going by rail. One quarry firm, however, still uses the branch occasionally as a private line although goods traffic officially ceased in 1968. Despite having closed to passengers in 1947, and again in 1949, the line has been used since 1985 for special trains for the Well Dressings in May and the Wirksworth Festival in September. *Authors' Collection*

Plate 233. One of the auto trains at Wirksworth in 1906 consisting of M&GN 4–4–0T No. 10 and ex parlour car No. 5, originally named Minerva. The locomotive is a hybrid with Johnson safety valve cover and smokebox door and M&GN brass dome with Salter safety valves. It appears to be in M&GN livery. *Authors' Collection*

Plate 234. Although the Keighley & Worth Valley Railway was conceived and financed locally, the Midland provided considerable assistance and the 1862 Act of incorporation gave the latter powers to purchase land and build the line. Construction started in 1864 and after several delays the line opened on 13th April 1867. Ingrow, seen here sometime after 1910, was the first intermediate station from Keighley.
R.C. Betts Collection

Plate 235. The terminus of the Keighley & Worth Valley line, Oxenhope, as seen in 1906. The lighter coloured portion of the station building nearest the camera was later addition. Of the posters in evidence, one is appropriately enough for Thomas Cook's excursions – Mr. Cook's first ever excursion having been on the Midland Counties Railway in 1841. Note the gas pipes running along the platform face.
R.J. Essery Collection

Plate 236. A view from the opposite end of Oxenhope station taken at the same time showing that at least two types of fencing were in use; that in front of the goods shed is of the wrought iron paling type whilst beyond the shed is vertical wooden paling. Although the line closed in 1962, it was saved by the Keighley & Worth Valley Preservation Society and reopened in June 1968. It has been beautifully restored and the stations evoke wonderfully the atmosphere of a Midland branch line. Oakworth station achieved immortality in the film "The Railway Children".
R.J. Essery Collection

Plate 237. The entire local population appears to have turned out at Grassington on 29th July 1902 for the opening of the Yorkshire Dales Railway from Embsay. As would be expected, the locomotive pulling the inaugural train towards the crowded platform is one of Johnson's ubiquitous 0–4–4 tanks. It is doubtful whether Grassington ever witnessed such a crowd again, much as the Midland's traffic manager would have liked it! When the line opened the YDR was still nominally independent and the picture shows an absence of Midland Railway poster boards. *Lens of Sutton*

Plate 238. A short while later and things at Grassington were much quieter, enabling us to see more of the station buildings. As the nameboard reads only Grassington, this photograph must have been taken prior to October 1902 when the station was renamed Grassington and Threshfield. *Authors' Collection*

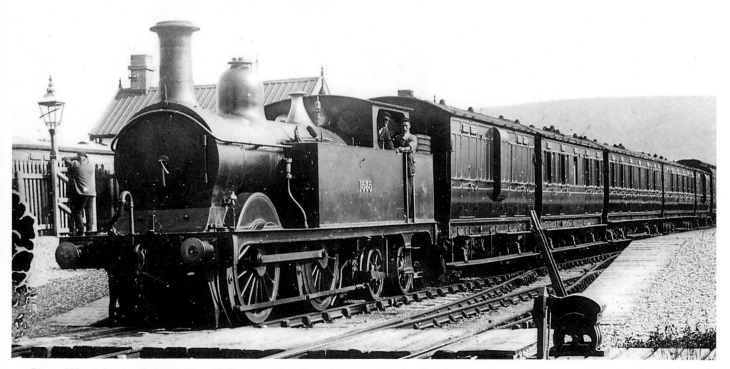

Plate 239. Johnson 0–4–4T No. 1535 was a familiar sight at Grassington for many years. It is seen here leaving with a 5 coach branch set and a clerestory bogie carriage, possibly a through coach, *circa* 1905. Since the previous two pictures were taken a fence and gaslamp have appeared in front of the loading bay. *L&GRP*

Plate 240. Stonehouse station on the Bristol & Gloucester line looking along the branch platform for the line to Nailsworth. There is a drawing of the wooden building in Peter Smith's "The Midland in Gloucestershire" (OPC). *Lens of Sutton*

Plate 241. At the other end of the branch was Nailsworth station seen here on a summer's day *circa* 1910. The branch was opened on 1st February 1867 and had three intermediate stations at Ryeford, Dudbridge and Woodchester. In 1885 a sub-branch opened to Stroud. *R.C. Betts Collection*

Plate 242. Nailsworth station building was an extremely attractive stone structure as this *circa* 1910 view shows. *Authors' Collection*

Plate 243. Coleford station was at the end of a short branch on the Severn & Wye Joint Railway. Originally incorporated as the Lydney and Lydbrook Railway in 1809, the Severn & Wye opened as a horse-operated tramway in June 1810 laid to 3 ft. 6 in.gauge. During a chequered lifetime the gauge changed several times between the limits of 3 ft. 6 in.and 7 ft. in various combinations, until in 1883 it finally became a locomotive-worked standard standard gauge railway. Passenger services were introduced in 1875. In 1879 it amalgamated with the Severn Bridge Railway and in 1894 was jointly vested in the Midland and Great Western Railways. The joint station was adjacent to a GWR one and there was a physical connection between the two, albeit involving several reversals. The station was closed to passengers on 8th July 1929.
Lens of Sutton

Plate 244. The Dursley branch was opened in 1856 as the Dursley and Midland who purchased the line and all plant following and agreement reached in February 1861.The branch, one of Britain's shortest, had only one intermediate station, Cam, on its 2¼ miles of single track. This view shows the approach to Cam station, the level crossing gates in the centre of the picture being at the end of the platform. The gates themselves were demolished by over enthusiastic locomotive drivers several times! Just to the left of the Thomas P.O. wagon is the Railway Hotel. The rest of Cam's amenities consisted of two sidings, a timber-built goods shed and a small red brick station building.
P. Smith Collection

Plate 245. Dursley station, seen here *circa* 1900, showing the attractive station building, much enlarged over the previous decade to provide more booking office facilities and a station master's office. The building being erected on the left of the picture is the beginning of R.A. Lister & Co's Churn and Woodware works, a concern destined to change the locality completely.
J. Guthrie Collection

TICKETS

The development of ticket types on the Midland Railway is exemplified by this account of the development of Midland Edmondson singles. When the Midland was formed there were first, second and third classes. It was also possible to purchase first and second class Express and Mail tickets which in some though not all, cases cost slightly more than the ordinary fares.

Some 12 years earlier, in 1832, the Government had imposed a tax on the railways of ½d per mile in respect of every fourth passenger, which in 1842 was changed to 5% of gross passenger receipts. The earlier arrangement particularly had generally encouraged companies to concentrate on first and, to a lesser extent, second class passengers to maximise their revenues, and those who paid third class fares often found that they could only travel at inconvenient times and sometimes just on goods trains. As railways developed, there was public agitation to improve the conditions of travel for the less well-off and this led to Gladstones' "Cheap Trains Act" which came into force on first November 1844. This stipulated that all passenger railway companies should run at least one train per day in each direction on all their lines calling at every station. The overall speed was not to be less than 12 mph, carriages were to be provided with seats protected from the weather and the adult fare was not to exceed 1d per mile. In exchange for this, the Government was to relieve the railway companies from paying taxes on all such fares. On the Midland, this new class became known as "Government Class", though on some early tickets it appeared as "Fourth Class".

The earliest Midland singles were of a very simple style common to most companies at that time, showing only the issuing and destination stations, the class and the serial number on the right hand side (1). Tickets also appeared with a code – thought to represent the destination station – between the two words forming the class line (2). It is not certain which of these two types preceded the other.

During 1859, the Midland reduced the number of classes, discontinuing local Express, Mail and third class facilities, which just left first, second and Government Class tickets.

By 1862, the typeface had been reduced so that a conditions notice could be included below the class (3), whilst two years later tickets were appearing with miniature repeats of the destination station under the conditions (4).

The next change, about mid-1867, saw the company's title added at the top of the tickets (5). This was followed in 1873 by the addition of miniature repeats of the issuing station and a serial number on the left hand side (6), which meant that tickets were now in a form where the essential information was on both halves and they could be bisected for issue to children. It will be noted that this particular example is of a third class ticket. This arose from a further change in classification during 1872. On first April, the Midland announced that it would be putting third class carriages on all trains and that passengers would be "booked and conveyed at Third Class Parliamentary Fares". In effect, this meant that Government Class had been re-designated third Class - the opposite of the 1859 situation. However, this change was not reflected immediately on tickets and some Government Class tickets were printed in the style of (6). Another point of note was that while fares remained at the Government Class level of 1d per mile, most were now subject to taxation under the provisions of the Revenue Act 1863 and subsequent Board of Trade practice.

In January 1875, the Midland went even further by abolishing second class facilities on all trains internal to its system. Indeed, this was even more startling for what it actually did was reduced first class fares to the old second class level of 1½d per mile and re-designate second class coaches third class, charging the latter's rate of 1d per mile. So both Government and second class tickets were discontinued during the currency of type (6).

By mid-1878, the company had radically transformed the layout of its tickets, with the journey details appearing in a much clearer form (7).

From first October 1883, the Government at last released the railway companies from paying taxes on all 1d per mile passengers irrespective of the classification used and, other than in certain local situations, third class fares were to stay at that level for another thirty-odd years. This, of course, had no effect on the printing of tickets. However, the Regulation of Railways Act of 1889 did bring some change. This stipulated that from 1st July 1890, the fare had to be shown on the faces of many types of tickets and principally on ordinary singles and returns. To a limited extent, the Midland seems to have anticipated this requirement as a few tickets showing a printed fare have been seen from 1885 onwards (8). However, this was not a universal practice and tickets in (7) and (8) appeared simultaneously.

About 1889, the company decided to repeat the printing of the class on each half of the ticket and again examples appeared both with and without the fares (9)(10). The ticket illustrated in (9) would have been supplied for the opening of Branston station on first October 1889. One direct consequence of the 1889

1   MAIL DERBY TO **DONCASTER** SECOND CLASS

2   NEWARK TO **LONGEATON** THIRD 5 CLASS

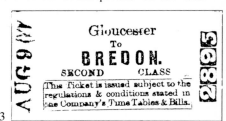

3   AUG 9 187 Gloucester To **BREDON.** SECOND CLASS This Ticket is issued subject to the regulations & conditions stated in the Company's Time Tables & Bills.

Act was that old stock were over printed with the fare and in some cases this involved tickets printed nearly 30 years previously (11).

By mid-1890, the fare as well as the class was being printed on each half of the ticket (12). The company now had a ticket which conveyed all necessary information on the face except the date of issue, which, because of the large serial numbers, had to be stamped on the back. The disadvantage of turning the ticket over to check it properly was overcome by reducing the size of the left hand serial number in order to make a date stamp in this position legible (13), a feature which became standard on all sub-sequent Midland prints. Tickets of this type were being issued late in 1892, but by the end of 1893 a new type had appeared (14). This had the title and conditions in a reduced typeface to accommodate the addition of an availability clause below the class. Tickets of this design then continued to be printed for almost 11 years and even then – commencing in late 1904 – the only variation was in the spacing of the conditions (15).

Having relegated the title to little more than part of the conditions for some thirty-odd years, the Midland brought it back to prominence during 1910 (16), though to do this it was necessary to condense the conditions into two lines.

By late 1912, the top portion of the tickets had been revised again to allow the inclusion of two large reference numbers (one on child tickets) (17). The significance of these has never been satisfactorily explained but the rule appears to have been:-

"1" - On all first class tickets, other than Day and Half Day Excursions and free passes.

"2" - On all third class tickets, other than Day and Half Day Excursion and free passes.

"3" - On Day and Half Day Excursions - both first and third class.

"4" - On first class free passes.

"5" - On third class free passes.

The change in style can be vividly seen from the consecutively- numbered tickets in (16) and (17). "B + B" after Eckington stood for Birmingham & Bristol, which was the Midland's way of differentiating the station from Eckington & Renishaw in Derbyshire. Whatever their function, the reference numbers had been discontinued by early 1920 and for a very short period, tickets appeared in the same format, but with the numbers omitted (18).

Following the outbreak of the Great War, all main line railways were placed under the control of the Railway Executive. The war effort made heavy demands on both men and materials and this led to a period of rapidly rising costs. As a result, from first January 1917 and fares were increased by 50%. Excursion trains, which had been somewhat reduced since the outbreak of the war, were withdrawn and so were many cheap fares. Initially, it became the practice to amend the fares by hand but it was not until early 1920 that tickets began to appear with the new "Actual Fare" printed on them. In a few cases, examples are known in the same format as (18), but in the majority of cases there was a return to the 1910 layout of (16). – See (19).

"Actual Fares" tickets were short-lived as from 6th August 1920, the Railway Executive further increased fares to 75% above pre-war levels. The new scale was identified on tickets as "Revised Fare" and again print in the formats of both (16) and (18) are known. An example of the latter type is shown in (20).

The level of costs began to fall during 1921 and in 1922, the Railway Executive decided that fares should be reduced to 50% above the pre-war levels from first January 1923 – i.e. to the January 1917 levels. This was too late for the Midland to be really concerned as the Grouping was to take effect on the same date. However, it did print quite a number of tickets showing the new fare scale of "(1–23)" and its own company title (21).

4

5

6

7

8

9

10

MIDLAND RAILWAY. This Ticket is issued subject to the Regulations & Conditions stated in the Company's Time Tables & Bills.
THIRD CLASS.   THIRD CLASS.
Upper Holloway   to
KING'S CROSS
U Holloway-King'sCross   U-Hollow.A-King'sCross

11

MIDLAND RAILWAY
Haverstock Hill   To
HIGHGATE ROAD
GOV'T   CLASS.
This Ticket is issued subject to the Regulations & Conditions stated in the Company's Time Tables & Bills.
Highgate Road   Highgate Road

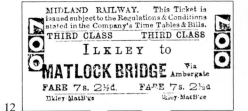

12

MIDLAND RAILWAY. This Ticket is issued subject to the Regulations & Conditions stated in the Company's Time Tables & Bills.
THIRD CLASS   THIRD CLASS
ILKLEY to
MATLOCK BRIDGE Via Ambergate
FARE 7s. 2½d.   FARE 7s. 2½d.
Ilkley-MatB'ge   Ilkley-MatB'ge

13

MIDLAND RAILWAY. This Ticket is issued subject to the Regulations & Conditions stated in the Company's Time Tables & Bills.
THIRD CLASS.   THIRD CLASS.
(A.)   LEICESTER   to
SYSTON
FARE 4½d.   FARE 4½d.
(A.)Leicester-Syston   (A.)Leicester-Syston

14

MIDLAND RAILWAY. This Ticket is issued subject to the Regulations & Conditions stated in the Company's Time Tables & Bills.
FIRST CLASS.   FIRST CLASS.
AVAILABLE ON DAY OF ISSUE ONLY.
Camden Road   to
KING'S CROSS
FARE 4d.   FARE 4d.
CamdenRd.-King's↑   CamdenRd.-King's↑

15

MIDLAND RAILWAY. This Ticket is issued subject to the Regulations & Conditions stated in the Company's Time Tables & Bills.
THIRD CLASS.   THIRD CLASS.
AVAILABLE ON DAY OF ISSUE ONLY.
Rushden   to
WELLINGBORO'
FARE 4d.   FARE 4d.
Rushden-Wellingboro   Rushden-Wellingboro

16

MIDLAND RAILWAY.
This Ticket is issued subject to the Regulations & Conditions stated in the Co.'s Time Tables & Bills.
THIRD CLASS.   THIRD CLASS.
AVAILABLE ON DAY OF ISSUE ONLY.
Wadboro'   to
ECKINGTON (B.&B.)
FARE 4½d.   FARE 4½d.
Wadboro-Eckingt'n   Wadboro-EckingtonB&B

17

MIDI   RLY.
issued su   conditions in the Co.'s   Tables & Bills.
THIRD CLAS.   THIRD CLASS.
Available on day of issue only.
Wadbro'   to
ECKINGTON (B.&B.)
FARE 4½d.   FARE 4½d.
Wadboro-Eck'tonB&B   Wadboro-Eck'tonB&B

18

MIDLAND RLY.
Issued subject to conditions in the Co.'s Time Tables & Bills.
THIRD CLASS.   THIRD CLASS.
Available on day of issue only.
Charfield   to
FISH PONDS
FARE 1s. 2d.   FARE 1s. 2d.
Charfield-FishPonds   Charfield-FishPonds

19

MIDLAND RAILWAY.
This Ticket is issued subject to the Regulations & Conditions stated in the Co.'s Time Tables & Bills.
THIRD CLASS.   THIRD CLASS.
AVAILABLE ON DAY OF ISSUE ONLY.
Woodhouse Mill   to
TREETON
ACTUAL FARE   ACTUAL FARE
W'houseM-Treeton   W'house M-Treeton

20

MIDLAND RLY.
Issued subject to conditions in the Co.'s Time Tables & Bills.
FIRST CLASS.   FIRST CLASS.
Available on day of issue only.
Ullesthorpe & Lutterw'th to
RUGBY
REVISED FARE 1/7½   REVISED FARE 1/7½
Ullesthorpe-Rugby   Ullesthorpe-Rugby

21

MIDLAND RAILWAY.
This Ticket is issued subject to the Regulations & Conditions stated in the Co.'s Time Tables & Bills.
FIRST CLASS.   FIRST CLASS.
AVAILABLE ON DAY OF ISSUE ONLY.
DERBY to
DERBY N. ROAD
FARE 2½d.   FARE 2½d.
(1-'23)   (1-'23)
Derby-DerbyN.Rd   Derby-DerbyN.Rd